Enemies Within

How the Church was Invaded by Unbelievers Vol.1

FIRST PRINTING

Billy Crone

Cover Design:
CHRIS TAYLOR

D1160733

To Rhett Falkner.

Thank you for being
one of the first people
to ever reach out to me
and pull me out of
the world of illusion
I was living in.

Unknowingly
I was once a slave to lies
But you showed me
the Way the Truth & the Life
Through Jesus Christ.
And now I am not only set free
but for all eternity.

Thank you for caring
and loving me enough
to tell me the truth.
For this I am
eternally grateful.
I love you.

5

Contents

Preface

I never thought I'd become a Christian, let alone a Pastor. Prior to getting saved, I'd be the first one to call out Christians and label them as nothing but a bunch of hypocrites. I would also state that Pastors were just great conmen who existed not only to brainwash people but to rip them off of their cash. Then I would mock God and Jesus and the Bible with my demonic occult mentality and warped New Age thinking denigrating God's Word as a mere book whooped up by man. All I can say today is, praise God for His great lovingkindness and mercy upon me. Therefore, as a former skeptic, scoffer and persecutor of the Church and Christianity, when I entered the Church and started attending Bible College and later Seminary eight weeks after being born again, I just kept my mouth shut. I soaked in as much of God's truth as I could because I felt, as a brand new Christian, who am I to say anything. I wasn't raised in the Church. I hardly knew anything about the Bible because I was the real hypocrite. I'd be the first one to tell Christians they were reading a book full of errors, yet I never even read it myself to see if that statement was true or not. Of course, upon later examination I discovered it wasn't true. But there I sat, week after week, just being a sponge, soaking it all in. However, it didn't take long to see there was something strange going on in the Church. Lots of worldliness, tons of it. People professing to be Christians were acting like the world, speaking like the world, loving this world, promoting the things, including the wickedness of this world. Now, I may not have been raised in the Church, but I could spot this deadly invasion a mile away as a former creature of the world. Unfortunately, this worldly invasion of the Church hasn't stopped right on up to this day. And now it has led to what God warned us about in the Bible nearly 2,000 years ago. The Great Apostasy. One last piece of advice; when you are through reading this book, will you please READ YOUR BIBLE? I mean that in the nicest possible way. Enjoy, and I'm looking forward to seeing you someday!

Billy Crone
Las Vegas, Nevada
2023

Chapter One

The History of
the Invasion

In this book, "Enemies Within: How the Church was Invaded by Unbelievers" we are going to break it down in segments and add some supplemental materials, that deal with it. This is also a great compliment to our Book of James study. What does the Book of James deal with? How to spot a phony Christian. You are going to see, not just stories from me but more importantly, scriptural examples. There are not just fakers in the church, but they have wormed their way up into positions of leadership in the seminaries, the Bible colleges, and the headquarters of mainline denominations. They are fakers, they are not Christians, and they expose themselves.

We are going to tear this subject apart, piece by piece and add some additional information dealing with the Supreme Court's decision on same-sex, homosexual marriage that took place about six years ago. We dealt with that subject immediately, the very next week at Sunrise Bible Church, and that study lasted for four weeks. This is going to come up again because the infiltrators, these fakers, who made their way into the church are not only denying basically, every cardinal doctrine of true Biblical Christianity, but they are promoting pluralism, all religions coming together. This is a denial of **John 14:6** that says Jesus is the Way, the Truth, and the Life, and nobody comes to the Father except by Him. Pluralism is what you need for a One-World Government. They are also all about inclusiveness, that anything goes.

They twisted the meaning of the word love, and somehow that became the rule that you can't say anything bad against anything. Actually, they are hypocrites themselves, because they come around with the rallying cry that we need to be more tolerant with one another. Tolerance. The hypocrisy is they say that we need to be tolerant and that's their number one virtue. But they don't tolerate me as a Biblical Christian? You know what they call that? Hypocrite! Right now, we are going to be in this passage, to show you that, unfortunately, this is nothing new. It's being repeated today and on a much more massive scale. Part of the reason why, is because of the last 30 years of the church growth movement.

If you are familiar with the church growth movement, it started here in the United States about 30 years ago. I was a brand-new Christian in Bible College, and I remember when it started to come into the church. The church growth movement was the idea that these people said it was a new way to do church services. They said, "What we need to do is go light on the Scripture, and really ramp up the music. We want lost people to come and feel comfortable, to like us, and to want to stick around." I was there, in Sacramento, when it was going down. It used to be an anomaly. Now it's the majority. But at the beginning that is how they sold it. Back then people were going, "That's crazy! You can't dumb down God's Word!"

What does the Scripture say? Pastors are to teach the whole council of God to equip the saints, which is, church services edifying one another, in God's Word. The exercising of the gifts and things that are for the church, not for the lost. But the way that they got people to buy into that lie was they said, "Oh no, we're still going to witness to them, what we'll do is get them to like us, get them to come into the church, and then maybe in a Sunday School class or some mid-week group study, that's when we'll tell them about the gospel." As soon as they came out with that excuse, people go, "Okay, I guess I'll try it." Extremely light, if any of it was Scripture, and if it was Scripture, it was just fluff. Scripture is not fluff, but they present it in such a fashion. Just saying stuff that you want to hear. They would teach Heaven. And Heaven's real, but there is also hell. God will forgive you by God's grace, and that's true, but He also wants us to turn away from sin. That's what they were doing. And then the Scripture really began to go away. The focus turned to you and feeling good about yourself. The music got ramped up more and more.

So, they got what they wanted. They got a bunch of lost people to show up. That's been going on for 30 years. The other reason the Church bought into that, was because they began to see the results. And the results were, these churches that bought into this lie, attracted a lot of flies, I mean a lot of people. You can attract flies with syrup, and that was what it was. A bunch of syrup. But we are supposed to be the salt and the light. So, then it was almost, dare I say the word, a lust that came over churches, pastors, and denominations, because these churches got big. This was the birth of mega churches. Then it was, "Wow! What are they doing? They've got to be doing something. How come we only have 75 people? We can't even get …"

And that is what I call the "cookie cutter method." Have you ever made cookies and used a cookie cutter? It's the same cookie every time you pop that baby down. It's an awesome cookie, the same one, consistency. So, basically that is what they did. It was a cookie cutter method. They figured out what these guys were doing, and they were going to do the exact same thing. And that got repeated everywhere. What they were doing was light on Scripture, if any at all, crank up the music, make people feel good, and guess what? It worked. There again, lost people like to feel good about themselves. They even like to feel religious with no conviction. They weren't convicted because they weren't teaching the truth. So, that became the new way of doing it. What started out as an anomaly, has now become the majority. Now, what's become the anomaly, is us, preaching the truth, the whole council of God, as crazy as that sounds.

And that is why we are in the mess we are in. I am convinced that the church growth movement was the first plank of attack of satan to give rise to what God warned would happen in the last days. The apostasy. These people have attracted so many, but they don't give the gospel. You may walk down the aisle, but what's their version of the gospel? God loves you; you just need to know that God loves you. That's not the gospel! So, these people going forward, getting dunked in water, becoming a member, were you even saved? Dare I say, NO!

When you have 70 percent, which is the latest statistic, of people who are professing specifically to use the term born-again Christian, and say that God accepts the worship of other religions, that there are other ways to Jesus, you're not saved. That's not coming from the world, that's coming from professors in the church. That tells you how much of the church is what? I don't care what you say. I don't care who you are. Again, this isn't just the people in the pews anymore. That's how it started. Now they have moved behind the pulpit, like what we have been seeing in the Book of James study. Now, they are in charge of seminaries, now, they are in charge of Bible colleges, and denominational headquarters. And it is spilling downhill.

What I want to show you, these are enemies within the church and they're not just enemies, they are non-Christians, and they expose themselves. Paul dealt with this.

Galatians 2:1-6: "Fourteen years later I went up again to Jerusalem, this time with Barnabas. I took Titus along also. I went in response to a revelation and set before them the gospel that I preach among the Gentiles."

Now notice that Paul also says elsewhere, "If anyone preaches to you any other gospel than the one that was preached to you, I don't even care if they claim to be an angel from God, let him be accursed." He said it twice. That is what these false teachers are doing. They are coming in with a different gospel.

Galatians 2:1-6, cont.: "But I did this privately to those who seemed to be leaders,"

Where were these people? Not in the pews, they were in leadership positions.

Galatians 2:1-6, cont.: "for fear that I was running or had run my race in vain. Yet not even Titus, who was with me, was compelled to be circumcised, even though he was a Greek."

These fakers had come in with a false gospel. They said you need Jesus, but you have to keep the Mosaic Law. That is not Scripture. People still do that, unfortunately, today. Not just with the Hebrew Roots Movement, but also Seventh Day Adventism, all those Christians say, "Oh yeah, we're Christians but you need to keep the Jewish Festivals, you need to worship only on Saturday to keep the sabbath. It's still going on to this day. Or maybe they may not be into that, but they say you need Jesus, but you have to be baptized. Baptism is good for you but that doesn't save you. The thief on the cross didn't have time to be baptized. You take something that is in remembrance, symbolic, like communion. Communion doesn't save you, but do people believe that taking communion can save you? Yes, it's the same thing that was going on in the early church. It's works. They're trying to say it's Jesus but works save you. No, the gospel says this. If anyone comes to you and says, "Jesus and" or "Jesus or" or "Jesus but," that's not the gospel. It's a false gospel.

Galatians 2:1-6, cont.: "This matter arose, because some false brothers (fake Christians) had infiltrated our ranks to spy on the freedom we have in Christ Jesus and to make us slaves. We did not give in to them for a moment, so that the truth of the gospel might remain with you. As for those who seemed to be important."

I don't care what position you hold, or if you have fourteen degrees, or graduated from the Bible this or the Bible that. I don't care if you are the top head guy of the University of the denomination of the … I don't care. You shouldn't put up with this for a second, as Paul said, if they start preaching another gospel...

Galatians 2:1-6, cont.: "Whatever they were makes no difference to me; God does not judge by external appearance – those men added nothing to my message."

Of course, what they were teaching was false. But how do you know if these guys are false? Paul tells you, but John is going to reiterate. They were in positions of authority; they were right there in the church. God doesn't look at the external position, clothing, verbiage, it's that you have and know the truth. I am specifically saying Bible colleges, seminaries, heads of denominations, pastors of churches, because you are going to see some that you recognize in the transcription of the next video. They are going to show you that they are not saved. They are fakers, false brothers, because they are preaching a false gospel. I don't care how long they have been in there, but the moment they come out and they divert off of Jesus, they didn't lose their salvation, they were never saved in the first place.

I John 2:19: "Dear children, this is the last hour and as you've heard that the antichrist is coming. Even now many antichrists have come. And this is how you know it's the last hour. They went out from us, but they didn't really belong to us. If they had belonged to us, they would have remained with us; but their going showed that none of them belonged to us."

So, somebody sits here and claims to be a Christian. And then they walk away from Christ, with Christ being the only way to Heaven, just a basic bare bones gospel message, I'm sorry, they lost their salvation. What does the Bible say? You never had it. You were a faker the whole time. You might have fooled the church. You might have fooled that person next to you, you might have fooled the congregants, you might have fooled the people that attended your Bible college, you might have fooled the rest of the people on the board at the denominational headquarters, but you didn't fool God.

But we will know. This is one of the acid tests. Jesus said by their fruits you will know. John says, here's fruit, if they walk away from Christianity, if they walk away from the gospel of Christ, they just showed that they were fake the whole time. I don't care if they were there for 40 years. It took awhile, but in one respect, I wish these fakers would leave the church. But here's the problem. Because of the church growth movement, they're comfortable in the church, the fake church. They've basically taken over, and now we are the anomaly. We're the weird ones.

I hear testimonies every week, phone calls, and emails from Christians around the world, and not just the United States and Canada. They say the same thing, I went to my pastor, I went to my Sunday School teacher, I went to my church and said, "Can we learn the rest of the Bible?" Seriously. A heart felt, respectful request and they are not only told flat out, absolutely not, along with a bunch of other excuses, but now it has moved to the stage where that person who asked to be taught the Bible, is kicked out of that church. This is where we are at now. Now they've infiltrated our ranks, so much so, that they have taken over. That is what we are going to see. So, let's begin that journey. How in the world did we get into the apostasy? Well, here we go.

Narrator: "What happened to the church? To the living, powerful, transformative, nation-shaking Christianity. What they are trying to do, is completely demolish western civilization and then to rebuild it in a just society."

A SOCIETY WITHOUT THE BIBLE

Narrator: *"How do you break down American Christianity?"*

1st speaker: *"I think the problem today, in our culture, is that many of our words have been co-opted and stolen and dumbed down and reversed."*

Narrator: *"Social justice is sold as something that it isn't. Critical race theory is sold as something that it isn't."*

BLM speaker: *"Whiteness has caused blindness of heart! Whiteness has caused blindness of heart!"*

Speaker #1: *"When you preach victimization, it always leads to vengeance and fights, us against them, me against you, I want my pound of flesh."*

Narrator: *"American churches today are where the universities were ten years ago. Pretty heavily Marxist, they're not quite there yet, but they are well on the way. Many of the seminaries and Bible colleges are definitely already there."*

PASTORS ARE BEING BRAINWASHED

Speaker #2: *"That message that they're going out and taking to the world is not that you need to repent of your sins and receive Christ. Instead, the message that you actually have is that they are under the weight of racism or sexism or homophobia and that we need to unify them together."*

Youth Pastor #1: *"I'm gay, I'm 29, I'm a youth pastor in New Jersey.*

Youth Pastor #2: *"I'm straight and I'm also a youth pastor in New Jersey.*

Youth Pastor #1: *"We're planning on sharing our lives together, for the rest of our lives, which we're not totally sure what that looks like. Obviously, Nick is straight, and he does plan on getting married. When he has a wife one day, she'll make those decisions with us."*

Speaker #3: *"The future damage of what we're doing now is just going to be enormous."*

Speaker #4: *"The entire fabric of family, personal wealth, private property, all those things are out the door and everything is the state. They believe the state is God. They don't define justice the same way as the*

Scripture. Oh no, it's going to be an equality alright and it's going to be a totalitarian, Marxist justice."

ENEMIES WITHIN THE CHURCH

This video opens up in a beautiful little town with a church in the center that has a tall steeple. As we go into the church there are pews on each side of the aisle leading down to the front of the church.

Cary Gordon: *"As I look at the history of the western church we see right now, it hardly resembles the empty shell of what it once was. My name is Cary Gordon. I am three generations deep in full-time Christian ministry. My grandfather, Dr. R.M. Mounts preached the gospel for more than 60*

years before he died. By the time that this movie was released, my own father, Dr. Larry Gordon will have preached the gospel of the Kingdom for more than 50 years. This is my 27th year of pastoring in Sioux City, Iowa. I understand ministry and I love ministry. I am a published author and I have conducted hundreds of media interviews concerning the intersection of faith and politics in the United States. I've even been known to pop up on occasion in documentary movies.

Why would a pastor of a moderately sized church built on top of a hill in the western Iowa cornfields do those kinds of things? Because I recognize the trajectory of western culture and I know what my kids and my grandkids are going to be facing, long after I'm dead and buried, if I don't do everything I can to fight against it. I am passionate about Jesus Christ. I am passionate about His beloved Church. I am passionate about the Bible. I love my congregation. I am passionate about the God-granted gift of the nuclear family. I love my wife. I love all of my six children. I like being a dad. Why? Because I'm a generational thinker as the Bible teaches all Christians ought to be.

Like the good men who drafted the U.S. Constitution, who included the words "and secure the blessings of liberty to ourselves and our posterity." Posterity being a fancy word for children and grandchildren. I see and understand the unavoidable consequences that past generations have brought upon themselves through error. I have studied history and reviewed obituaries piled up in the tombs of lost empires. I love America with all of my heart. I know that something is terribly, terribly wrong with western civilization. I can hear the death rattle. I can see the handwriting on the wall. I have heard this question asked by every stripe of man and woman on both sides of every political debate of every social controversy. What on earth is going on? What has happened to our society? The question everyone should be asking right now is, what happened to the Church?"

During a church service:

"How's everybody doing? Can you see what this is? This is a puzzle. It's a 35-piece, ABC floor puzzle for ages 3 and up. What I am going to do this morning is, I'm going to ask you to allow me to say a few things you've already heard. I've given you some puzzle pieces, but today I'm going to start snapping them together, So, you're going to need them. When you get a puzzle piece, you don't say, 'Oh, that's nice, I don't need that anymore.' No, you need these puzzle pieces. You need to take them again in your hand and let me snap them together and by the end of the service, if you'll let the Holy Spirit help you, I think you are going to see something fresh, that you haven't seen before.

We'll come back and talk about puzzles in a minute. We do live in a puzzling time, don't we? June 29th and 30th, 2010, Opinion Dynamics conducted a scientific national poll, and it revealed that 78 percent of Americans believe the founding fathers would be unhappy with our condition as a nation today. In a chilling recent survey, and when I say recent, about three years ago. Fifty-eight percent of respondent millennials, now that's you persons in their middle 20s to about 40 years old, right in there. Fifty-eight percent of them said they did not want free markets in America. They don't want capitalism. They overwhelmingly said they preferred socialism, fascism, or communism. You can lump all three of those categories together, they don't agree on things, but they do agree on this. They are statists, the state gives permission for the individual to exist.

What did the founding fathers believe? They said, 'No, that is wrong! The individual person created in the image of God gives permission for the state to exist.' So, here's the question. How do you go from living in a country where a huge supermajority at one time apparently cared about what their founding fathers would think to a great big super majority that firmly believe that the founding fathers were completely wrong? And we need to be communists. How do you do that in eleven years? Over the last three and a half years this has been the question that we've been preparing to answer as a movie crew. How do you go from point A to point B so quickly? What is going on right now, in our country, in our own cities is puzzling."

"Speaking of puzzles. When I was a kid, and I'll never forget it, we would go over to my grandmother's house and one of the things we would do when we got bored, she would say, 'Pick a puzzle' and so we would go over and select something and snap it together. When you looked at the box top you could see what the puzzle should look like when it's fully assembled. But something happened. Somebody had scrambled up the box tops so for an entire afternoon we were just frustrated, trying to put this puzzle together, because we were looking at the wrong box top while trying to snap together the right pieces. The journey like the one that we're engaged in to create this documentary film, is really similar to that in many ways. As we've traveled across the United States, we've met

with so many people, and have conducted so many hundreds of hours of interviews. Each one of them has given us a significant piece to this puzzle.

But there was one interview in particular at the very beginning of the journey that proved to be very significant, because this man had the correct box top view of what we were trying to assemble."

Trevor Loudon: *"I think a lot of Christians need to understand the heritage of the United States, the actual representative government that founded America comes out of Mosaic Law. When Moses was leading the people out of Egypt he was constantly besieged by complaints, and people coming to him, driving him crazy. So, he said go amongst you and choose representatives, which they did. That cut down Moses's workload quite considerably. Then when the United States was founded, it was founded on the concept that human rights came directly from God to the people, who could then choose representatives to form a government, which would protect those rights.*

So, do you think such a system might have enemies? Do you think all the tyrants of the world might be very upset at a system whereby the right came from God, and bypassed the rulers, and went straight to the people? Even before the Bolshevik revolution, American communists and socialists were plotting to bring this country down. One of the very first communist fronts formed in America was the Methodist Federation for Social Action.

The Methodist Federation of Social Action was formed by Professor Harry Ward, Jr. from Union Theological Seminary, and he spread communist doctrines right through the Protestant Churches in America. Now the

enemies of America understood that America was a very strong country, and that the churches were the backbone of America. So, how are you going to destroy America? You have to do it from the inside, and you have to get inside the churches. I had a friend who was a communist investigator. He was a former communist party member. He said the softest touches, the easiest people to manipulate by the communist party were Protestant Pastors, because they were primed for it.

Well, there was a man called Joseph Fletcher who taught at the Episcopal Theological College at Harvard University  *for many years. He was a long-time activist, and he was the man who helped set up Planned Parenthood. He helped to set up the Right to Die Society. His wife worked very closely with Margaret Sanger, the founder of Planned Parenthood. And in his later years he became a leader of the field of bioethics, which is basically how to justify abortion and euthanasia. In 1966 he wrote a book called 'Situational Ethics' and it took the Christian world in America by storm. Because it was all about, there is no fixed morality, your morality depends on the situation, the circumstances that you're in. So, for people who really wanted to abandon the old morality of the Old Testament, this was a great justification. This gentleman was one of the most influential Christians in the United States, but for most of his career he was an active supporter of the Communist Party USA. He worked very closely with the Communist Party in Boston. He was a member of the World Peace Council, which was the main Soviet front at the time. He worked for Stalin. This man worked for Stalin, one of the greatest butchers the world has ever seen, yet he became one of the most influential theologians in America. The man who transformed the church to accept the idea that ethics were flexible.*

After he wrote that book, after a lifetime of communist and theological activism. He abandoned Christianity, became an open atheist, and advocated for things such as the forced euthanasia of children up to the age of nine or ten."

Cary Gordon: *"So, what you're saying is, that one of the most influential Christian theologians in America became an avowed atheist publicly and was supporting eugenics, like what you see in the book Mein Kampf, written by Adolf Hitler?"*

Trevor Loudon: *"Absolutely, he held human life in no regard. Abortion was perfectly acceptable; euthanasia was perfectly acceptable in the communist society. You are not a human being; you are a cog in a machine. Life is only worth what it can produce for the collective."*

Cary Gordon: *"After I first met with Trevor Louden, I felt like I really had a pretty good broad view of what was really going on in the United States, but I still had to snap the pieces together."*

John Harris, Author and Podcast Host of Conversations That Matter:

"There is a history to the movement we're seeing now and here's what happened. In the early 1970s, Christianity, Evangelicalism in particular,

was going down a path to social justice. It started in campus radical movements mostly of the 1960s. Richard Mouw, in the reform tradition ends up getting radicalized in college and started to walk away from his Christian faith, but he reads the 'Uneasy Conscience of

Modern Fundamentalism.' He finds out that there's a way to base his new left ideas on a Christian framework. The premier institution for neo-evangelicalism is what Carl Henry came up with, it was Fuller Theological Seminary. So, this seminary started changing their focus from understanding the Bible and communicating to souls, to now transforming social structures, creating a new movement.

People like Ron Cider, Jim Wallace, John Alexander, Sharon Gallagher, Samuel Escobar and the list goes on came together in 1973 and they put together what was called the Chicago Declaration on evangelical social concern. Here is a portion of the Chicago Declaration:

'We must attack the materialism of our culture and the maldistribution of the nation's wealth and services. We recognize that as a nation we play a crucial role in the imbalance and injustice of international trade and development. Before God and a billion hungry neighbors, we must rethink our values regarding our present standard of living and promote a more just acquisition and distribution of the world's resources.'

They were academics. They were people who worked for the government. They were elites. Working class people rallied around Jerry Falwell, Pat Robertson, and people like that."

James Robison: *"If you think our solution is political you too have been deceived. Don't you commit yourself to some political party or politician, you commit yourself to the principles of God, and demand those parties and politicians align themselves with the eternal values in this book, and America will be forever the greatest nation on this earth."*

John Harris: *"The moral majority, religious right, formed and they took the nation by storm and stole all the headlines. So, it was an academic elitist movement, the social justice movement. They ended up going to other places, mostly in academia. So, they are now teaching. They're under the radar, they're not getting the headlines the religious rights are getting but they're still present. They didn't all die. They didn't go away. They kept doing what they were doing, and they taught it in places like*

Wheaton College, Fuller Theological Seminary, and the next generation of academics and pastors have been taught at their feet."

Jim Simpson, Author of Who was Karl Marx: *"The communist goal is to overthrow every government and run the world. We are its main competitor and given that Christianity has been our chief source of strength throughout the centuries, that absolutely had to go. That had to be discredited, undermined, smeared, and utterly destroyed before they could present us with their alternative.*

Michael Hichborn, President, Lepanto Institute: *"The communists have always been looking for inroads, so about the 1920s, and this was after the soviet revolution in Russia, they started infiltrating seminaries. They targeted various religious orders. They targeted the Franciscans. They targeted the Benedictines. But what they primarily targeted, were the Jesuits and because the Jesuits were very, very highly educated, they used a lot of their education, and their highly developed philosophy in order to hide what they were really teaching."*

Trevor Loudon: *"Bella Dodd, who was a member of the American Communist Party, back in the 30s, she was in the teacher's union in New York. She talked about how she had helped to bring 1,100 young communists into the Catholic Church."*

Michael Hichborn: *"She said that by the time she got out, which was about 20 or 30 years later, she had seen many of those young men raised to the rank of Bishop and even Cardinal."*

Cary Gordon: *"So what we're seeing happen right now has already happened before and it's happened in the Catholic Church."*

Michael Hichborn: *"Without a doubt. And one of the things that I think cannot be emphasized enough is that the primary mode of promoting socialism within the Catholic church and how you're seeing it in the Protestant community is through social justice initiatives."*

Trevor Loudon: *"What is the communist front? What is a socialist front? It's an organization that purports to do one thing but has a significant number of leaders involved or enough leaders to actually push it in another direction."*

Cary Gordon: *"I booked a flight to Washington D.C. to attend my first CPAC. I will never forget the words that I read in a book I happened to have along with me in my lap to pass the time of travel. Apparently, the Chinese Academy of Social Sciences, the communist regime, had been studying America for about 20 years. They were studying to figure out what it was that was ultimately responsible for the unprecedented success of the United States. An official of the Atheist Communist Chinese Academy of Social Sciences said the following words in summary of their 20-year study of the west. And I quote:*

'We studied everything we could from the historical, political, economic and cultural perspective. At first, we thought it was because you have more powerful guns than we had. Then we thought it was because you had the best political system. Next, we focused on your economic system. But in the past 20 years we've realized that the heart of your culture is your religion. Christianity. That is why the west is so powerful. The Christian moral foundation of social and cultural life was what made possible the emergence of capitalism and then the successful transition to democratic politics. We do not have any doubt about this.'

Consider the irony, the Chinese communists are looking at the correct box of the jigsaw puzzle of the West while a growing majority of Americans are looking at the wrong one. Is justice an important word for a Christian?"

Everett Pipe, Former President of Oklahoma Wesleyan University: *"Absolutely. If it's social justice, that's justice that's defined by society. If it's Biblical justice, it's justice that's defined by God."*

Brad Dacus, President, Founder of Pacific Justice Institute: *"What God does in His word, He holds us accountable as individuals. Social* *justice wants to obliterate that and instead hold governments and people accountable for the choices and decisions of other governments and other people."*

Kevin McGary, President of the Frederick Douglass Foundation of California: *"Social justice is a euphemism for Marxism. Fairness, the same basic outcomes. You know, if you're a billionaire then I should be a billionaire. And so many of our churches, especially our urban churches, are encouraging people to look at things of this world and bemoan the relative position that we have within our community and look at all these other communities."*

Trevor Loudon: *"It's sold as a way to improve people's lives. To give people more security. To help people. It's not! It's a way to enslave them. It's a way to mislead them, and it's a way to give certain unscrupulous people way more power than they ever should have."*

Cary Gordon, with his church congregation: *"Two short years after the communist Chinese study was released to the public, they shared it everywhere. Another communist regime in the far east led by the infamous, Kim Jong-un, rounded up as many as 80 Christians. Took them into stadiums. Packed the stadiums with ten thousand men, women and children, tied them to posts and killed them with machine guns. Forced men, women, and children to watch. Why? Because they had a Bible. They were caught with a Bible in their house. Two of the largest communist regimes on planet earth had recently acknowledged that the Bible was and is the source of the strength of the free market, arch enemy, America. One recognized that an honestly read, interpreted Bible, is so anti-Marxist, so anti-socialist, this book is so anti-status, so anti-communist that anyone found with it in their possession should clearly be executed. They needed to be executed publicly in front of the whole nation to discourage anyone else from reading its dangerous anti-communist comments. Meanwhile in floundering America your clergymen and growing chorus are showing less honesty and integrity than communist authorities on the other side of the ocean by telling the next generation of American activists that Jesus was a socialist. And that socialism is a*

27

legitimate tool of Christian compassion. They have switched the box tops. They're lying."

Michael O'Fallon, Founder and CEO of Sovereign Nations: *"We're hearing pastors saying these things. We're hearing them using terms like intersectionality, critical race theory, systemic racism, etc. Then you're bringing that into the church, Black Lives Matter and so forth. Normally it would be the church that is in opposition to what's happening and instead what you see is a melding of things."*

Albert Tate, Pastor, Fellowship Church, Pasadena, California: *"Lion King, has everybody seen the Lion King? You've got Simba, a lion, Timon, the meerkat, Pumba the warthog. What in the world are they doing together? How is it they are kicking it and have become a beloved community? Well, Simba, the lion, has to become a vegetarian. Whites have to become a vegetarian to their privilege, and sacrifice privilege for the sake of the whole."*

Kevin McGary: *"White privilege is a misnomer, especially for all of us in the United States. Everybody born in the United States is privileged."*

Bishop E.W. Jackson, Founder of The Called Church in Chesapeake: *"I'm supposed to buy the idea that a person is my oppressor, and I am their victim because their skin is one color, and my skin is another color. That's the message it's trying to send."*

Cary Gordon: *"Where does the term white privilege come from?"*

Trevor Loudon: *"It came from the Maoist movement. It came from Ted Allen and Noel Ignatiev; they were two communist party members who moved from the pro-Russian camp into the pro-Chinese camp, and they invented the term white privilege. Go back to the Maoist revolution, the cultural revolution in China in the 60s. Remember the pictures of the people who would be in front of big sessions, and they'd have a sign around their necks, 'Capitalist.' You know, because their father was a business owner. They could never escape the taint of capitalism and the* *whole idea was to create a new culture where people could be much more easily manipulated. Because you created this enemy, and the enemy was the capitalist. Well now the enemy is the white person who has white privilege. So, everybody's out there competing amongst themselves to denounce those with white privilege."*

COMMUNIST PROPAGANDA – WHITE PRIVILEGE

Chanequa Walker, Theologian, Columbia Theological Seminary:
"Whiteness is a dysfunctional system. It is a pathology that poses a danger to the fabric of our democracy if left unchecked."

David Platt, Pastor McLean Bible Church, Washington, D.C.: *"I want to sacrifice more of my preferences. As a white pastor, I need to grow. I do not want to speak from the Bible on issues that are popular among white followers of Christ while staying silent in the Bible on issues that are important to non-white followers of Christ."*

Jackie Hill Perry, Woke Mother and Speaker: *"I feel like until all white people, and I say all white people, look within themselves and say God, where is the deceitfulness of my heart. Where have I bought into the narrative that all black people are criminals. Where am I treating my neighbor not as better than myself. Where am I assuming that I am superior and they are inferior because of the color of my skin.*
I am sorry I have grieved you because they're made in your image and also, we have to understand that white guilt is not repentant.

Gary Gordon: *"In America it is very clear to me that the millennial generation, in particular, is very frustrated and even angry as they try to put the broken pieces of our once great society back together again with a completely inverted vision for what American is supposed to look like when they get finished. This time, it's different. This time the puzzle box*

top was swapped deliberately. And it was the Christian church in an effort to appease the spirit of the age. They swapped the Biblical vision for a just society, with an artificial, humanistic, relativistic false gospel designed to please the flesh of sinful men. Rather than confront the problem of sin, that resides in the ruined soul of every sinner, and provide the solution for its necessary punishment, which is the powerful work of the cross of Jesus Christ and what it really means. Instead of that, in an effort to attract, and coddle, and pacify the wicked without confrontation of God's law against man's sin, they changed the truth into a lie."

Dr. Russell Fuller, Former Professor at Southern Baptist Theology:
"At Southern seminary, when I first came it was a transition period. I came five years after Al Mohler became president of Southern Seminary. There's a case in my department, in the Old Testament department, where we hired someone. We either hired him in very late 2017 or very early 2018. So, it was fairly recent. He believes that the Old Testament teaches mythology. Mythology!"

Cary Gordon: *"So none of it's true?*

Dr. Russell Fuller: *"None of it's true. It's just poetic."*

Cary Gordon: *"And Al Mohler hired this guy?"*

Dr. Russell Fuller: *"Oh, yes, and the Dean knew all about this and I wrote up some notes on this and said, 'Look at this, this is a serious problem, we should not be hiring someone like this.' He knew this information, and he still hired him."*

Cary Gordon: *"And so denying the inerrancy of scripture is something that is routinely happening in the school where you've taught."*

Dr. Russell Fuller: *"Now they won't say that out loud. No, no, no, they will say that they can sign the statement, don't worry. There is a statement that we have to sign affirming right inerrancy. People will say anything in order to teach in an institution. This goes on all the time, it really does."*

Ray Moore, Executive Director of Exodus Mandate: *"This is a very unusual controversy that we're having with the social justice movement because historically it started when we've had a false doctrine of false teaching coming into the church. It's usually been against the trinity. They deny the Cardinal Doctrines. These are not doing that, at least now, but they have a socialistic neo-Marxist social policy."*

MARXISM SPREADERS

Alexander Jun, Professor, Azusa Pacific University: *"We hear that a lot. That sounds awfully socialist, that sounds kind of neo-Marxist. I don't know if that's Biblical. One I think we have a misunderstanding of what Biblical is. When we address racial reconciliation, maybe there is something that Marxists and others have talked about that may apply, if all truth is God's truth."*

Darryl Ford, Pastor IKON Community Church, Georgia: *"There are no questions, that there are things that are absolutely true, but we can't just look at absolute truth in a vacuum. We can't possibly understand truth if we don't understand the lay of the land and if we don't understand the power differential."*

Jarvis Williams, Professor, Southern Baptist Theological Seminary: *"I don't think it's possible in a Christian context to talk about reconciliation without likewise talking about justice and we are working together, living together in love and spirit and power, love that means we care about things like economic equality and these sorts of things. That doesn't mean you're justified by economic quality, equality, but that does mean that the gospel transforms us holistically."*

Guest speaker: *"Jarvis Williams basically preaches a critical race theory infused gospel where he takes critical race theory principals, and then he takes the Bible, and he finds parallels, and he creates his own racial reconciliation. That's what he calls it. He said it's part of the gospel, but it's not. If you read what he actually says, it requires you to do things like, you know, take down white Jesus, and platform minorities, because they're not being platformed, or if you are white you have to shut up and listen to other perspectives, because you're not able to ascertain the truth the same way. He incorporates this all into his racial reconciliation doctrine.*

You have Walter Strickland of Southeastern Baptist Theological Seminary, who in the past few years has preached a liberation theology. In fact, he even said on campus, that the gospel itself is to love God and your neighbor. That's not the gospel, it's the law. So that is a classic liberation theology category error. Liberation theology is Marxism with a Christian veneer."

Trevor Loudon: *"It was a 100 percent invention of the KGB, but the idea is that salvation is not personal, salvation is created even on earth. And you do that through socialism. The utopia on earth so completely twisted Christian doctrine, but they kept the Christian terminology"*

Cary Gordon: *"You mentioned earlier Professor Cone."*

Bishop E.W. Jackson *"He comes out of a school of high criticism of Scripture. He's one of these people whose decided that his intellect is a better barometer of good and evil, right and wrong, than the Bible itself. His whole viewpoint is that the only way that you can understand the gospel and the Bible is to see it through the lens of racism."*

Cary Gordon: *"This teaching is not isolated only to him. It has found its way into almost all of the seminaries and Bible colleges in the United States."*

James T. Roberson, Pastor, Bridge Church, New York: *"We have to have a whole reorientation of the way that we do seminaries. Race must be central to understanding God in America because racism is central to America. Racism is not a personal experience. Racism is a system that we're all experiencing. I am feeling its detriment. White folks are feeling its benefits. There's a great book, 'The Color of Compromise, by Jemar Tisby. Read that."*

Cary Gordon: *"Have you seen the infiltration of the social justice gospel in your school?"*

Dr. Russell Fuller: *"Absolutely, I've seen a real shift at Southern Seminary. Let's say, in the last five or six years there's been a real shift towards the left. So, again, we have guys teaching post-modernism, social justice, and of course critical race theory. And you hear all the buzzwords. This is coming from the very top. So, you have people like Matt Hall who* *is now the second person. I mean, he teaches textbook critical race theory using all the buzz terms, using all the concepts."*

Cary Gordon: *"Which is total heresy."*

Dr. Russell Fuller: *"You cannot take a secular doctrine, combine it with Scripture, without distorting and perverting the gospel. It's absolutely impossible. He'll say, 'I don't believe in critical race theory, but go look at the videos, they're readily available. And by the way, in a meeting, Al Mohler, himself, started using that very vocabulary and he meant it. He talked about the problems of whiteness, white privilege, and then he started talking about systemic racism and then finally one of the last things he said was, 'Marxism has insights.''"*

Cary Gordon: *"Al Mohler said that? Marxism has insights?"*

Dr. Russell Fuller: *"That's right and remember the context. He's already using the word whiteness as if he's accepting it. At another faculty meeting earlier in that year he said, 'Listen, I don't agree with all the solutions that critical race theory offers for the racial problems, but they are seeing the problems correctly.' Therefore, what he is saying is there's a problem with whiteness. There's a problem with white privilege. There again, he's agreeing with how they're seeing the problems of society. We need to see things how the Bible sees things, not critical race theory."*

Randy Adams, Executive Director of Northwest Baptist Convention: *"The whole CRT intersectionality issue which has become huge in Baptist life is puzzling to me because as believers we understand that all people are created in the image and likeness of God, and we are held responsible individually for our sin. We're not classified in groups and this whole thing about classifying people according to identity to me is antithetical to Scripture."*

Cary Gordon: *"If you're like me, these kinds of discoveries are painful to accept. We had hoped to find evidence to the contrary. But then Professor*

Robert Lopez reached out to us and provided even more incriminating evidence.

Robert Lopez, Former Professor at Southern Baptist Theological Seminary: *"It was clear that they wanted to change the curriculum in a certain direction, and I couldn't quite figure out what was going on. They had removed the person who was the historian in the department, so we lost the history. Now they were seriously shaving off the literature. As they were slashing all of those classes they threw in new requirements. People had to take critical thinking and world view, a lot of philosophizing, a lot of theorizing, and then they had to take this thing called, 'Meaning, vocation and flourishing,' which is really just a blend of economic philosophy with Christian language laid on top of it. But all of it, in a sense, extensions of what they were hearing during chapel sermons, what they would be hearing during Sunday School, what they were hearing on their Wednesday Bible studies. It's all kind of general theorizing about how they should look at the world, but not with content."*

Cary Gordon: *"Is another way of saying this is that they were removing objectivity and replacing it with subjectivity?"*

Robert Lopez: *"Absolutely, one hundred percent. You go from teaching history and literature of different kinds of people around the world, where you are fixed on what actually happened and what great people from those cultures said and then moving to theory, which is always abstract. It's always muddled, it's always nebulous, as you say. Then you move to critical theory which is where having been stripped of all of the knowledge about what people said and what actually happened, students are then told that they should apply their critical thinking skills to, what?*

So, they're just sort of critically thinking, theory, so it all becomes person A cites person B, who cites person C and I'm going to talk about my opinions on what this person said about what that person said about what that person said. It becomes derivative, it becomes very subjective, and it becomes really a waste of people's energy. And they're not being given the classical education that they thought they had signed up for when they go to a seminary of that kind. So then from critical theory, it's just a hop, skip, and a jump to critical race theory, where now you're going to be talking about these different racial or ethnic subjects totally in abstract and model-based relationships as in oppressor versus oppressed.

I think that I can do a lot more by teaching someone for instance, African American writers of the 19th Century, than forcing them to theorize how oppression works or how white privilege works. Do you see what I am saying? That's the direction the curriculum was going in.

Cary Gordon: *"How in the world could seminaries, of all things reject facts, history and objective truth? How could these once great schools become compromised so quickly? How did this deception of secular humanistic thought get into the minds of our top thinkers?"*

I'm thinking fakers infiltrated these institutions on purpose and began to take them over. That's exactly what happened. You wonder why we are promoting the seminary education here at Sunrise on Monday nights? It's because of Tyndale, which is my alma mater, which was started by Dr. Mal Couch in Fort Worth, Texas, back in the day. He taught at some of these other big seminaries. He deliberately started Tyndale because he could already see they were starting to slide and that was at least 30 years ago. That's why we offer it at our church.

Also, closing in the gap of education, what we also have on Monday, is our homeschool group. Get your kids out of the sewer pipe, not only this baloney in so-called church services, but get them out of the sewer pipe of the school system that's just reinforcing this baloney. You can come here, get hooked up and learn how to homeschool. Be a part of the co-op and things of that nature. This is why we are doing this, because this is what's going on.

One thing I want to back track really quick on, just to clarify, I don't think this is what they were meaning because later you're going to hear a testimony of the guy that admits that he came out of Catholicism, and he wasn't saved. But if you recall, there's a section there where they talked about how the Catholic church got infiltrated with this stuff too. Just to clarify and make sure we're all on the same page, Roman Catholicism is not Biblical Christianity. It's a works based, false gospel, you have to keep the sacraments in order to be saved. That's Jesus and the sacraments.

It dawned on me as we were going through this. I have been here at Sunrise Bible Church for 11 years now. It may sound kind of weird, but out of the original group when I first came here, I think we are down to 7 people. Some of it was, I think, we were dealing with a lot of fakers. But what you may not know, our somewhat recent history of Sunrise and why we turned into Sunrise Bible Church. It was because of this stuff. We lived it live. It was back in 2017. Sunrise was started back in the late 50s, 60s at our old location as a Southern Baptist Church. Southern Baptist, used to be a pretty solid Christian denomination. But not anymore. What happened was, as a church, as we're going through the Scripture, in 2016 I started getting reports. Pastor Billy, did you hear about the latest decision from the leadership of the Southern Baptist Church? No.

And this is when it all started to go downhill, and we began to do our own investigation. The first thing that we learned was the mosque issue. In 2016, the Southern Baptist leadership jumped on board to defend the building of a Muslim Mosque in New Jersey. It's still in print, they're not hiding from it. That was the first thing. Can we support this? We're Christians, right? Well, here is what it says:

"Southern Baptist Convention Supports Mosque, Draws Criticism 06-21-2016 Caitlin Burke.

"The Southern Baptist Convention is coming under fire for filing a legal document arguing for the construction of a mosque by an Islamic society in New Jersey. The paper offers legal arguments in support of the local Islamic society's efforts to build a mosque in Bernard's Township, New Jersey, despite the opposition of the local planning authority. 'A Muslim Mosque cannot be submitted to a different land-use approval process than a Christian church simply because local protesters oppose the mosque.' it says according to The Economist. At the SBC's annual meeting last week in St. Louis, Missouri, the Ethics and Religious Liberty (ERLC) arm of the SBC came under fire for supporting the construction of the mosque. 'I move that all Southern Baptist officials or officers who support the rights of Muslims to build Islamic mosques in the United States be immediately removed from their position within the Southern Baptist Convention.' said Messenger John Wofford, with Armorel Baptist Church in Arkansas. SBC's Russell Moore defended the decision to support the building of the mosque during a meeting of the ERLC. 'What it means to be a Baptist is to support soul freedom for everybody,' Moore said. 'Brothers and sisters, when you have a government that says we can decide whether or not a house of worship can be constructed based upon the theological beliefs of that house of worship, (5/4/22, 10:57 AM Southern Baptist Convention Supports Mosque, Draws Criticism | CBN News) then there are going to be Southern Baptist churches in San Francisco and New York and throughout this country who are not going to be able to build.' The ERLC was joined in signing the amicus brief in support of the mosque by the Becket Fund for Religious Liberty, International Society for Krishna Consciousness, National Association of Evangelicals, Sikh Coalition, South Asian Bar Association of New York, and Unitarian Universalist Legislative Ministry of New Jersey."

We need to help people. That's not Biblical help. You need a sandwich, you're hungry, I'll feed you. You need a shirt, you need some clothes, I'll get you some clothes. But I will not support you building a mosque that is then going to be used to propagate anti-gospel, false teachings that is going to lead people into bondage and straight into hell. I can't do that as a Christian. Then what made it worse was that the ERLC jumped on board with all of this. So, that was what came out in 2016 and we're like, wait a second. I'm not going to take what I see on the internet. You can't trust everything there, so I called the headquarters. I wanted to ask them if this was really what they were going to do. I called and called, and they would not return my phone calls. For four weeks, I'm the squeaky wheel. Every week I'm trying to contact them. I just want to know what is going on, if it's true. They never called me back but after a month they sent me an email and basically said, "Yep, that's what we're doing." They justified it, we're not backing down, too bad.

That was a watershed moment, and it went downhill fast from there. At that point we immediately stopped any finances. I can't give a penny to these people doing this, but let's do our homework and make sure. The next thing was the money trail. You could not get any records from the executive board of what the salaries were. They wouldn't give it to us. There are apparently signed disclosures that you can't disclose what these people make. Yet we're supposed to be transparent as Christians, as churches but we can't know what you make?

And it wasn't just that, then it led to the missions debacle. We began to do the research on all this money. The way the Southern Baptists work, which I always found was very strange, you as a church don't get to decide where or what missionaries you want to support. All you do is cut them a big fat check every month and they do the "work" for you. That's how it works. I've always found that strange. But what are they doing with all of these millions and millions of dollars, every year, that are just cut to them? You would think it was going to missions. No, what we found out was it flip-flopped. About 80 percent of it was going to headquarters overhead and maybe about 20 percent was actually going to the mission field. Typically, you want it the other way around, 20 percent to overhead and 80 percent to whatever the purpose is. So that was backwards.

So, then we found that other non-Southern Baptists, like Fundamental Baptist Churches that had way less finances, way less majority of congregants, they were blowing these people out of the water, with way less money. And then they began to say, "We need to withdraw missionaries from the field." Now there's something going on with that. Now this sounds like something out of a science fiction story, and it just keeps getting worse. This all happened in a process of about six months.

Then we discovered this little egg. They merged with the United Nations. Oh, that's why they are supporting this Universalist, One World Religion tolerance. This was some of the investigations that I had done and told some of the other pastors to check it out, it's true. They are now under the headship of the United Nations, the ERLC. If you do the research, under the Ethics Religious Liberty Commission, at that time, when we were dealing with the Muslim Mosque issue, there was a guy named Russell Moore. The guy before him, that Moore replaced was Dr. Richard Land. Dr. Land had made a deal where he came under the headship of the United Nations. He put the ERLC into what's called an NGO, a non-governmental organization so they could work with the United Nations.

So, I went to the UN website and looked to see if the ERLC was hooked up with the UN and sure enough, they were listed there. And they were in good standing. So, I asked, "What do you have to do, in order to be in good standings, with the United Nations as an NGO?" The answer was, "You have to abide by, you have to promote and support the teachings of the United Nations." Now, here's where it gets really bad.

Just before we were about to jump ship, I found out that this guy, Augie Boto, the Vice President of the executive board, was coming to Las Vegas. So, all the Southern Baptist pastors in Las Vegas got to meet with the Vice President of the executive board. There was a Q&A where you could ask the guy questions. I'm thinking I don't have a lot of time, but I'm going to make the time. So, we're at the meeting and he's answering questions. I raise my hand and say, "I've got a couple questions for you." And I brought up this UN thing. I asked him, "Were you aware that Dr. Richard Land put the ERLC under the head of the United Nations, number one, and number two are you aware of what you have to do in order to be in good standing as an NGO with the United Nations? Can you explain that?" He looked me straight in the face and said, "Well, that's the first I ever heard of that."

Two things immediately popped in my brain. If that's true, what kind of a board doesn't know that somebody put you on the headship? No wonder things are messed up. Or dare I say, you just lied straight to my face. Either one is not good. So, we left and then the church became Sunrise Bible Church, not Sunrise Southern Baptist Church. At that point we said we're jumping ship, we're not going to any other denomination, because at this rate, who knows if they're going to go south too. We're going to go on our own, we're going to follow what the Bible says. Headship under Christ, Bible alone and we're going to have elder/deacon rule and we're going to call ourselves Sunrise Bible Church, because that's what you're going to get when you come here. That's it! So, that's when we made the jump. Just to explain the history.

So, we've lived what you have seen on the video, live as a church. I just wanted to give you that because I had a feeling that a lot of you don't know our history, even though it wasn't too long ago, but I felt in the context you should know that. But I asked him another question and we'll get into it in the next chapter. Even bigger than the UN, all the other pastors were flipping up their hands, going like, "Hey, what do we do about homosexuals coming to the church?" I wasn't the only one, there was a bunch of them, because they were concerned. They are using any excuse to accuse us of intolerance, and they sue churches out of existence because they can't handle the legal bills. The church goes belly up. It's just a tactic to take down churches. There's a concern. So, the pastors were literally, honestly looking at the vice president of the executive board. "What do we do? How can we protect ourselves? What are some practical legal steps with your knowledge as the headquarters over this whole denomination? What do we do to protect ourselves in case they come after us? We don't want to wait until the hammer drops. We want to be prepared." As a shepherd you need to know. You know what he said? "You just need to love these people. I know some homosexuals. I knew a homosexual once and I got to share the gospel with him." And he just dropped it like a hot rock.

And then I raised my hand for the next question. But I kid you not, right after that UN question he said, "Well it's break time, let's take a break." That's the kind of baloney that's going on. I left the morality for last because that's what we are going to get into in the next chapter. These guys are not only promoting a false gospel, social justice, whiteness, and all that but it's going to get worse. You're going to see even more. David Platt, who was the head of the North American Missions Board, Southern Baptist, did you know he's apologizing for his whiteness? You're going to see that they've also twisted the Biblical definition of love and now their version of love is to accept anything and everything. And this is what is being preached behind the pulpit.

Chapter Two

The Twisting of Biblical Love

In our last chapter, we saw the invasion of what's going on with this social justice system. This perversion of the Scriptures, and basically what we have been learning in our study of the Book of James, is that fakers are no longer in the pews. Now they have moved up into positions of leadership, and they are controlling things. We saw they are doing it in seminaries, Bible colleges, headquarters of denominations, and that all spills downhill. If they are raised in that baloney, then they go into the churches, and it gets disseminated. That is why we're in the shape we are in today.

In this chapter we are going to deal with the next aspect of the invasion. They're in, but now they're perverting the Word of God. We are going to see that they are also perverting the Biblical view of love. Their version of love has now become the excuse. It's all twisted. It's not God's definition of love. And it opens the gates to any kind of behavior, i.e., homosexuality. So, we are going to dispel that.

Now, before we go there, let's take a look at one of the passages that they pervert. Now why didn't I just go with **John 3:16**? Because if you just read **John 3:16**, which is what they do, it's wrenched out of context. That is what they do. They don't look at the whole context of what's going on. When you truly understand Biblical love, who God is, as love itself, it's radically different than what's being presented in a lot of so-called churches today.

John 3:14-18: "Just as Moses lifted up the snake in the desert, so the Son of Man must be lifted up, that everyone who believes in Him may have eternal life. For God so loved the world that He gave His one and only Son, that whoever believes in Him shall not perish but have eternal life. For God did not send His Son into the world to condemn the world but to save the world through him. Whoever believes in Him is not condemned, but whoever does not believe stands condemned already because he has not believed in the name of God's one and only Son."

Now, even in **John 3:16** that should be a clue of what is the proper understanding of Biblical love. God gave His Son Jesus, out of love, so that you wouldn't perish, contextually not just die. The wages of sin is death, that's where death and suffering come into the world. But ultimately, we deserve to perish and go to hell. But God loves us. We don't have to go to hell. Through His Son we get the polar opposite. We get eternal life.

Here's where they take it out of context: "God did not send His Son to condemn the world." They say God just loves everybody and anything. He loves you so much, He's not going to condemn you. You can do whatever you want to do, whatever lifestyle you want. No! Of course, He doesn't condemn, because you're already condemned. You're already under the wrath of God. You already deserve to go straight into hell. But God's Biblical love says, "I'm going to do something about it. I'm going to send my Son, so that you won't perish and go straight into hell, which is what you deserve. I've already done all the work. All you have to do is believe on what He did. Receive it by faith."

Now that's love. But that's not what's being preached today in churches. Let's take a look at that twisted view.

Cary Gordon: *"How in the world could seminaries, of all things, reject facts, history and objective truth? How could these once great schools become compromised so quickly? How did this deception of secular humanistic thoughts get into the minds of our top thinkers? One missing puzzle piece is antinomianism. That's a mouthful."*

Antinomianism means: The heretical doctrine that claims Christians are exempt from the obligations of moral law summarized in the Ten Commandments.

Cary Gordon: *"Antinomianism comes from the Greek meaning lawless. In Christian theology it is a pejorative term for the teaching that Christians are allegedly under no obligation to obey the divine laws of ethics or morality summarized by the Ten Commandments. Many believers mistakenly believe that the gospel is like a 12-piece puzzle for preschoolers. But it's definitely a ten-thousand-piece puzzle much larger and much more magnificent than they can see. They have the wrong picture in front of them.*

What is the gospel then? When you hear the word gospel, what picture comes into your mind? What's your vision of the gospel? Your vision, what you actually believe the gospel is, is so important! If you just read the Bible, it is very clear that the real gospel is probably not what most people think that it is in the west. It is a fact that most Americans believe to be the sum total of what they mistakenly call the gospel is just a really tiny shrunken down fragment of what it really and truly is.

It's not that the tiny truth they mistake as the whole gospel isn't true, it's just that it's insufficient. It's too small. It's too selfish. They believe that the gospel is three words, "God loves you." I'm here to tell you that God does love you and that is certainly true, but with equal force I want you to listen to me when I tell you, the real gospel of the Bible simply should never be reduced to those particular three words.

Dr. Douglas Bankson, Senior Pastor, Victory Church World Outreach Center: *"You know Paul made a very, very important statement when he* *said, 'Behold the goodness and the severity of God.' Because if we don't see both of those sides, you know, people have a tendency to fall into the ditch and there's a ditch on both sides of the road. We have to be careful with that. We have to be doctrinally pure. Which Paul himself said, 'Until the law came, I knew no sin.' So, God brought that to show us right from wrong.*

The law is not evil. It proved that we were. And it showed us, it's like building a house. I built my own home years ago. If you take a level and you put it against a crooked wall, you don't say the level is off, you say the wall is off. Right? But what we've done is we've changed the definition of things, such as, 'God is love.' We have changed it to 'love is God.' Then people's own personal definition of what love is begins to form their definition of who God is. It's the other way around. God defines love like the level defines the wall, not the other way around."

Cary Gordon: *"In the gospel of Matthew, the Book of Matthew. Is the subject of the love of God ever mentioned one time?"*

Dr. Douglas Bankson: *"It's not."*

Cary Gordon: *"In the gospel of Mark, is the love of God mentioned, even once?"*

Dr. Douglas Bankson: *"No."*

Cary Gordon: *"In the gospel of Luke, this is three of the four books, is the subject of the love of God mentioned one time in the entire gospel of Luke?"*

Dr. Douglas Bankson: *"That is not the focus of it."*

Cary Gordon: *"In the gospel of John, everyone knows one verse, **John 3:16**. But nobody seems to be able to quote verse 15 or 17. In that chapter, **John chapter 3**, what is the real subject and the emphasis of that chapter because it does mention the love of God? 'For God so loved the world,'* which is wonderful, 'that he gave His only begotten Son that whosoever should believe on Him would not perish and have everlasting life.' But it's just mentioned. What is the larger context of that chapter?"

Dr. Douglas Bankson: *"Well, of course, Nicodemus, who was the ruler of the Jews, which again was their political system. He came to Jesus privately because he knew what was popular. He knew He had something so he came and said, 'What must I do to be reconciled to God?'"*

Cary Gordon: *"To be reconciled?"*

Dr. Douglas Bankson: *"It's being reconciled to God and so Jesus said, 'You have to be born-again.' You cannot reconcile yourself. You're not a good enough person. It's because of these things that dealt with the depravity of man and the condition we were actually in. It's the doctor saying you have terminal cancer, and you must do this, or you will die."*

Cary Gordon: *"So, John Chapter 3, gives the consequence for not accepting what God lovingly did through Jesus Christ, which is the wrath of God. Is it fair to say, Matthew, Mark, Luke, and John are the gospels. The love of God is clearly not the emphasis of the pure gospel? And if we over emphasize a subject, God in His divine wisdom did not emphasize, we therefore are under emphasizing what? The Law of God."*

Dr. Douglas Bankson: *"Yes. In the beginning was the Word and the Word was with God, the Word was God, and He came full and grace and truth."*

Cary Gordon: *"That means the Old Testament was made flesh in Jesus Christ. So, if we're to vilify the Old Testament and say we don't need it anymore, you're actually talking about some part of Jesus."*

FALSE DOCTRINE – ANTINOMIANISM

Andy Stanley, Pastor, North Point Community Church, Georgia:
"You are not accountable to the Ten Commandments. You're not

accountable to the Jewish Law. We're done with that! God has done something new."

Bishop E.W. Jackson: *"You can't have justice without God's law because His standards are absolute and that's why communism is so dangerous. Because once you say there is no God, then anything I do in the cause that I am committed to is okay.*

And that's exactly what they believe, anything. You want to see murders, torture, everything imaginable, separate man completely from God and watch to see that there are no limits to depths of depravity to which we will sink."

Cary Gordon: *"I've noticed no one stops talking justice. We still want justice. Even though it's not possible to have justice without law. What is the law that they've made to replace God's Law?"*

Everett Piper: *"It's the subjective rather than the objective. It's feelings rather than facts."*

Cary Gordon: *"When law and love are discussed, is it best to juxtapose the two against each other?"*

Everett Piper: *"No, they're the same thing."*

Cary Gordon: *"They're the exact same thing?"*

Everett Piper: *"Right, you can have legitimate love without honoring some sort of law."*

Cary Gordon: *"Would you say that love is the most popular topic in every pulpit in America?"*

Dr. Scott Stewart, Senior Pastor of Agape Church: *"Love wins."*

Cary Gordon: *"Everyone talks about love all the time and yet do you believe that most of the church is even properly defining what love is?"*

Dr. Scott Steward: *"No."*

Cary Gordon: *"You have to have the Ten Commandments to really understand love."*

Dr. Scott Steward: *"You have to, because the Scripture tells us that, we know, in First John it says, 'This is the love of God that you keep His commandments.' And then it goes on to say, which I think is beautiful, 'His commandments are not burdensome.' Yet my entire life, all I have ever heard is that the commandments of God are weighty and burdensome and problematic. We need to get rid of them."*

Cary Gordon: *"Rather than see the New Testament as a continuation of what God was already doing right. But now through Christ. What I hear a lot of ministers doing is they're pitting the New against the Old. Literally everything in the New Testament, under that view, becomes relativistic."*

Dr. Scott Steward: *"Yeah."*

Cary Gordon: *"You can shape the New Testament to literally teach anything you want, yet you make love the only law and it's primarily just a feeling."*

Dr. Scott Steward: *"You can make any Scripture say anything you want to if you remove it from its context and you redefine terms. If you redefine terms, then you can make the Bible say anything you want it to say."*

Michael Hichborn: *"Marxists will take what is already being used in the church. They'll empty it of its meaning, so they'll take away what its actual definition is, then they'll refill it with a new meaning or a new interpretation. Sacrifice is the very basis for love. But what the Marxists will say is that love is affection. They think that the way to approach love or the way to define love is to show affection for somebody, and also for the homosexuals. They say if one man loves another man, as long as they're celibate. Well, wait a minute. Stop. You're not defining love in the same way. You're saying that it's possible for them to have kind of a romantic interest in each other and that's not proper. That's not right. It's disordered but they're now calling it love."*

Cary Gordon: *"The year I was born, 1973, seemed to put a bow on the turmoil of the 1960s. The obtuse and arrogant United States Supreme Court elevated themselves to the rank of Roman Caesar via the illegitimate opinion of Roe v Wade. Trouncing a plain reading of the United States Constitution and the Organic Law of the Declaration. But that wasn't the only horrible thing that happened the year I was born. On another front, a closeted homosexual coup d'etat of the American Psychiatric Association took place and reached its zenith when a majority of gay men snuck into voting positions and voted to remove themselves from the infamous list of psychiatric disorders. Declaring them perfectly mentally fit in contradiction with more than 100 years of clinical science."*

The American Psychiatric Association: *"Homosexuality is not a mental disorder and thus there is no need for a cure."*

Cary Gordon: *"So those two events of abortion and perverted sexual activism created a chain of events that have led us to now. A millennial culture who claims they were born gay, even though science says that they weren't, right after declaring that they were not born any sex at all. Even though science says that they were. Who knew that was any such thing as*

51

gender fluidity until like a year ago? No one had ever conceived of such a thing. This is such a groundbreaking discovery that the poor scientists have no earthly idea how to tell the public that gender fluidity has zero impact on the biological realities between human legs. But even if they do try, and who knows if they actually will try, will they get sued for discrimination and hate? Will they be bigots like the rest of us?"

Trevor Loudon: *"If you look at who founded the modern gay rights movement in this country, it was a man named Harry Hay. He founded the Matashine Society and other radical gay groups in the forties and fifties.*

He was a very active communist party member. He left the communist party because he could do more good for the cause without the communist party label. He remained a communist till the day he died. He is absolutely the father of the modern gay rights movement. Now you have to understand with these movements, it's not about the movement. The issue is not the issue, the issue is the revolution. How do you break down the American family? How do you break down American Christianity? One of the best ways to do it is to turn homosexuals into an accepted minority that must be atoned to. That must be both accepted into your society and be even above normal. They must have more rights than anyone else."

FALSE DOCTRINE – HOMOSEXUALITY

JD Greear, Former President, Southern Baptist Convention: *"It would appear that quite a few other sins are more egregious in God's eyes than homosexuality. Lynn Wilkin, who's one of our favorite Bible teachers here and who's actually leading our women's conference, she says, 'We ought to whisper about what the Bible whispers about. We ought to shout about what it shouts about. The Bible appears more to whisper when it comes to sexual sin compared to his shouts about materialism and religious pride."*

Trevor Loudon: *"Now the LGBTQ Movement as they call it these days has made huge inroads in Christian churches in this country. Many Christian churches had gone from holding homosexuality as a sin to welcoming homosexuals into their church and apologizing for their past unaccepting behavior.*

John Harris, Author and Podcast Host of Conversations That Matter: *"At an ethics and religious liberty commission, Al Mohler repented, he used that word, for denying same sex orientation."*

Cary Gordon: *"What?"*

John Harris: *"He believes that homosexuality is an innate orientation."*

Cary Gordon: *"He repented for taking a Biblical position on sexual behavior?"*

John Harris: *"Yes."*

Cary Gordon: *"He repented for being Biblical?"*

Al Mohler: *"One of the embarrassments that I have to bear, and I have written on some of these issues now for nearly 30 years, and at a couple points I have to say I got that wrong. We have to go back and correct it. Correct it by Scripture. Early in this controversy I felt it quite necessary, in order to make clear the gospel, to deny anything like a sexual orientation and speaking at an event for the National Association of Evangelicals twenty something years ago, I made that point, I repent of that."*

Dr. Russell Fuller: *"If you go back to like 2005, he said that the notion of sexual orientation was a key thing in really promoting the homosexual agenda in America. The idea that people are born gay, basically, if you accept this, you're giving up the farm is what he was saying."*

Cary Gordon: *"I was particularly shocked. How could a man with this knowledge of Scripture, that has written X, Y and Z, that is so good, do this? Jettisoning his Biblical view of homosexuality and accepting a postmodern view of homosexuality?"*

Dr. Russell Fuller: *"Now he charges the church with homophobia, with a form of homophobia, that the church has lied about homosexuality. Al Mohler has made a major change in his view on homosexuality. He promotes people like Sam Allberry."*

Ray Moore, Executive director of Exodus Mandate: *"The old Al Mohler would fire the new Al Mohler. I'm 75, I've got two seminary degrees and I'm theologically trained. But he was somebody that I did look up to. It was very, very disappointing and shocking to a high degree to realize that he had real involvement in this."*

Dr. Robert Lopez: *"One of the things that they made very clear was that I was not to talk about that issue, and I was not supposed to say anything* *that would appear like criticism of Al Mohler or Russell Moore. Which meant that I really had no way of countering the poor theology that they were spreading. My mother and father were breaking up just as I was born. She was gay and she got into a relationship with a woman after the breakup. My mother just didn't bond that strongly with me. So, I felt very much neglected and alone and I developed very effeminate mannerisms when I was young.*

I was easy prey, you could say, for some predators and I was first brought into homosexual activity at the age of 13. When I remember this now, I also remember that this happened with a lot of alcohol. The older boys got me drunk. I started to believe what everybody had told me, which was that people are born gay. They can't change. If you try to change you are going to kill yourself. So, I assumed that I must have wanted it. This must be who I was, and I just gave up on the idea of trying to be with girls. Then from that point on I was really deep in the gay world up until the age of 28.

I got cancer and I called my father. At that point I got to know my dad. I remember being in the attic of that house where my dad and my grandmother lived and looking at the family albums. It was all men and women with families. And I realized that that was who I was. So, I got out of that lifestyle. I got up enough confidence to start asking girls out on dates. Then I met my wife. I was Catholic at that time, but I didn't really come to the Lord until 10 years later. Then I realized that I needed to completely surrender to Christ to get rid of all the lingering habits from that lifestyle. So, I got rid of all that.

At the heart of the gay question, is that the community is full of abuse. It's not all physical sexual abuse but it's emotionally abusive. Because you are lying to people. You're telling them that they are born that way and because that myth doesn't hold up because so many people get out of the lifestyle. But they have to set the clock earlier and earlier as to when to reach people with that message to recruit them in. So, now they're in kindergartens, they are in 5th grade classes.

You are given the message that if it's who you are, and you're not going to go along with it, you will kill yourself. When you think about how traumatic that statement is for a young child. It's not right when someone

tells them that this is your future, you're gay, you were born that way, and you can't leave. Now even the Bible is telling you that you can't leave. That is so wrong! It's a ticking time bomb. Because ultimately the truth will come out. Eventually people will realize that the gay movement lied, and that people are not born gay. People can change. People are going to realize that the Bible is clear, the Bible was right, and it all made sense from the very beginning. There were two types of bodies designed.

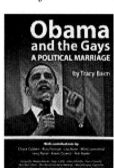

There was male and female, and they were made for a certain design and a certain purpose. Once people realize that truth, ultimately, all of these people who played all of these games to try to minimize it or to camouflage it or try to accommodate it or to succumb to it, they all lied. They were all part of the big lie.

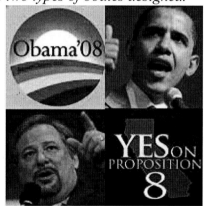

And what was the lie? You took a Biblical word, a Biblical concept, i.e., love, and you completely twisted it out of its context. There's actually four different Greek words for love.

Stergo- Love my car

Phileo – Love my wife
Eros – Sexual emotional passion
Agapao – Self-sacrificial action purely for the
      benefit of another person

That's why the Bible says God demonstrated what true Biblical love is by doing something sacrificial. He sent His Son to die for our sins. You can go back to John 3:16, "For God so 'agapao.'" He did a self-sacrificial action, purely for the benefit of another person, i.e., He sent his Son, Jesus Christ, to die on the cross, to live the perfect life in our place, fulfilling the law that we could never have. And then through that, we could be rescued from perishing in hell. That's just a taste of Biblical love. But do you see how twisted it's become?

So, let's take the next few chapters and dive down deep into what exactly is God's Biblical love. With that context in mind, you'll be able to better compare God's love with what the world now defines as love.

Chapter Three

God's Love is
Merciful Compassionate & Kind

There's an invasion going on. And once again this is a perfect complement to our study in the Book of James. Fakers are mentioned all through the Bible, false prophets, false apostles, false teachers and false brothers. But it's not just in the Bible, it's going on today. That's why we are in such apostasy. We have already seen that these fakers are coming out now, and admitting that they are atheists, bringing in this socialism, communism, and their twisted perverted view of God's love. They have taken over the seminaries, the Bible colleges, the denominational headquarters and of course, even the churches. It's spilling downhill on purpose.

They are destroying the church because they are taking God's truth and perverting it, twisting it. One of the ways they are doing this is the understanding of God's love.

Now we are going to look at the aspects of love. In these passages we are only going to hit one aspect. Basically, if you use this analogy, like if you have a diamond, a diamond has many different facets. You have a Biblical term called love. God is love. That is what we are going to see in this passage. But there are many different facets that God gives us, and when you get all of them together, all facets, it really amplifies. You really appreciate Biblical love even more.

I John 4:7-10: "Dear friends, let us love one another, for love comes from God. Everyone who loves has been born of God and knows God. Whoever does not love, does not know God, because God is love. This is how God showed His love among us. He sent His one and only Son into the world that we might live through Him. This is love, not that we loved God, but He loved us and sent His Son as an atoning sacrifice for our sins."

So, the Biblical context is of course, God is love and He demonstrates that love in one aspect by sending His Son as an act of sacrifice for our sins. Why? Because if sin isn't dealt with, you get what you deserve. You perish and you go to hell. Now what do they say? "God just loves you. You need to accept that God loves you and He loves anything and everything you ever do and there's no consequences." What? That is completely wrenched out of its context!

So, let's get a better Biblical understanding of that. Now again, the first aspect is multifaceted. We are going to take a look at God's love. He demonstrates that by giving us something called, "Mercy." Mercy means to bring help to the afflicted. Now here is a word that has been wrenched out of the church vocabulary today, "wretched." Mercy means to bring help to the afflicted or the wretched. Churches today have actually changed the words of "Amazing Grace." *"That saved a wretch like me."* No, we can't say that. That's not loving. That's their definition of love. That word will destroy your self-esteem. *"That saved a person like me."* That's what they're doing. It's sick, it's gross. It means to bring help to the afflicted or the wretched, to show compassion, withholding what we deserve. So, what do wretched sinners, people who have sinned against a Holy and Righteous God, deserve? We deserve to perish, **John 3:16**, and go to hell.

Out of merciful love, what did God do? He (verb) "agapao," He sent His Son as an atoning sacrifice for our sins so He can show mercy to us, and we don't get what we deserve. We deserve to go to hell but then He gives us something completely opposite. Now this is just one of the five aspects of His love in the Scripture. When you get it, it's just like, wow! It makes you appreciate what He's done. They have cheapened, they have ruined, they have lied to people, they're destroying lives with their twisted view of love.

Now people don't plead for mercy. They want justice, and their justice isn't even Biblical justice. They messed up love, they messed up justice. And then we'll add another word to it, social justice. "I deserve" something. They don't plead for God's mercy. In the gospels, the sinner goes to the temple and as he is beating his chest, what is he saying? "God have mercy on me, a sinner." But what's the religious Pharisee saying? "Well at least I'm not as bad as him." It's that kind of attitude. But mercy is when you understand what you deserve, and you are pleading for God's mercy. People don't do that anymore. They demand justice. That God owes them something. Society owes them something. They have even ruined this aspect of justice.

Now, I've said this before. Don't ever ask for God's justice. Because if we got what we justly deserve, what would we get? We would perish and go to hell forever. And rightly so. But this is where God's mercy comes in. They say, "You owe me something, I deserve a raise, I need a new house, I deserve a car, I deserve good health just like everybody else." It's all about you and what you deserve. You deserve a break today. Remember the McDonalds commercial? "You deserve a break today." If McDonalds were Biblical, they shouldn't say, "You deserve a break today," but "You deserve to go to hell today." That doesn't sell cheeseburgers, apparently.

But that's the point. They don't plead for God's mercy. They demand justice and even their term "justice" is just as messed up. "You owe me!" Now let's take a look at God's mercy, in the context. God doesn't owe us anything! The fact that He would self-sacrifice His Son for us, to rescue us from what we justly deserve. Whoa! Now that's love! Let's break that down. The merciful love of God. He shows that by giving his enemies, and that's the key word here, we were considered enemies, He gives His enemies a palace in Heaven instead of a pit in hell. There are three characteristics of who we were. What was our standing before? Does God owe us anything?

Romans 5:10: "For if, when we were God's enemies, we were reconciled to Him through the death of His Son, how much more, having been reconciled, shall we be saved through His life!"

So, does God say that before we were saved our identity was that we were His best buddies? We were His friends? You have people that are actually saying that Jesus Christ had to die on the cross because we were so worthy. No! What does He say? "You were God's enemies." So, Biblically, God sent His Son, and it's your choice. If you as an enemy of God, standing outside of Christ, if you don't want to receive God's merciful love through His Son, Jesus Christ, and be saved, what are you going to get? You're going to get justice, alright. And it's going to be Biblical justice, not social justice.

The first thing you are going to get is, you're going to go straight to hell. In **Matthew 25**, we're told hell was originally created for the devil and his demons. But since mankind has rebelled like the devil and his demons, even after God made a complete way out of the mess, make the wrong choice and to hell you will go. Why in the world would someone deliberately choose hell, is beyond me. Take a look at the Characteristics of Hell.

CHARACTERISTICS OF HELL

Place of Thirst: (Luke 16)
Place of Worms: (Mark 9)
Place of No Return: (Luke 16)
Place of Remembrance: (Luke 16)
Place of the Wicked Dead: (Luke 10)
Place of the Wicked Demons: (II Peter 2)
Place of the Bottomless Pit: (Luke 8)

Place of a Burning Waste Dump: (Matt. 23)
Place of Outer Darkness: (Matt. 8)
Place of Fire: (Rev. 20)
Place of the Lake of Fire: (Rev. 20)
Place of Eternal Fire: (Matt. 18)
Place of Unquenchable Fire: (Mark 9)
Place of Everlasting Punishment (Matt. 25)
Place of Eternal Condemnation: (Mark 3)
Place of Eternal Judgment: (Heb. 6)
Place of Everlasting Destruction: (II Thess. 1)
Place of Weeping and Gnashing of Teeth: (Matt. 13)
Place of Torment: (Luke 16)
Place of Eternal Torment: (Rev. 20)

The torment never stops, and you can't get out! "You owe me this, I deserve this lifestyle." What? You should be pleading, "Oh God, have mercy on me, a sinner. I'm an enemy God. I'm in a heap of trouble. And then you come across the mercy of God. The love of God. "Even though there is no way I can get out of that and that's justice. That's what I deserve? Yet you sent your Son, "agapao," a self-sacrifice to get me out of this and it's complete? He did all the work and all I have to do is say, "Yeah?" I'll take that. I want that. I believe in that. I'll put my faith in that. That's all I have to do?"

And it's not just that He saves you from that but in His mercy what does He do? He gives you the absolute polar opposite. What did it say in **John 3:16**? "That you would not perish but have eternal life." The exact polar opposite. So, we deserve to go to that place called hell, that's the justice. But the merciful love of God kicks in, and through His Son Jesus Christ, if you'll just accept that, I'm going to give you a place called Heaven.

CHARACTERISTICS OF HEAVEN

The Dwelling Place of God: (Psalm 2)
The Dwelling Place of Angels: (Matt. 18)

A Heavenly Country: (Hebrews 11)
A Holy Place: (Isaiah 57)
A Place of Eternal Rest: (Rev. 14)
A Place of Eternal Joy: (Rev. 7)
A Place Without Wickedness: (Rev. 22)
A Place Without Darkness: (Rev. 21)
An Eternal Paradise: (I Cor. 12)
A Place with Streets of Gold: (Rev. 21)
A Place with Gates of Pearls: (Rev. 21)
A Place with Foundations of Precious Gems: (Rev. 21)
A Place Without Sin: (Rev. 21)
A Place Without Tears: (Rev. 21)
A Place Without Mourning: (Rev. 21)
A Place Without Pain: (Rev. 21)
A Place Without Death: (Rev. 21)
A Place of Absolute Purity: (Rev. 21)
A Place Filled with the Glory of God: (Rev. 21)
An Everlasting Place: (II Cor. 5)

Just like hell, once you get there you aren't getting out. Praise God, if you go through Christ, you get to go to Heaven. That place is the exact polar opposite and that lasts forever too. And we don't deserve it. If you want justice, you go to hell. If you want God's merciful love that He made a way through His son, "agapao." His self-sacrificial action and you had nothing to do with it. You were His enemy and yet He did it anyway. "You deserve hell, but I'll give you Heaven and all you've got to do is say yes."

Once you understand Biblical love, you realize that these guys are in a heap of trouble with God for their perverted version of love.

R.A. Torrey: *"If you in any way abate the doctrine of hell, it will abate your zeal."*

Why? Because when you understand that we all deserve a pit in hell, yet out of mercy, God will give us a palace in Heaven, it's kind of hard to keep your mouth shut about it. Why? Because that's what happens when you truly understand the Merciful Love of God.

I'll never forget during my internship; I had this pastor, and he was doing this funeral. The plea was basically this: the person he was doing the funeral for didn't know Christ and you know he's not in Heaven. He was kind of stumbling through his words. But it's not just they're not in Heaven, they're in hell. I call it the silent "h" word in the church today. How can you appreciate truly what Christ has done out of His merciful love, sending His Son, if you don't understand what He saved us from?

The second act of merciful love is that He give you a body of perfection instead of a body of pain.

Romans 5:6: "You see, at just the right time, when we were still powerless, Christ died for the ungodly."

So again, what were we considered in the eyes of God prior to getting saved? Was it the godly ones? The good ones? No! it was the ungodly ones, right? And so, if people refuse to be reconciled to God through Jesus Christ and instead remain ungodly, what do they deserve for that kind of behavior?

Again, the choice is theirs. If they don't want to receive the mercy of God, then the justice of God declared they just earned a body of pain. And why anybody would choose that is beyond me.

One guy says, *"For a moment, let us try to imagine what it would be like to die and go to hell. Try to imagine that for every single moment, throughout all eternity, a time without end, every inch of your body will be in absolute pain.*

It will be like having scalding, boiling water poured over your body every single second. You say to yourself, 'Surely the pain will subside!', but it never comes. Your body will have an eternity without rest or relief.

It is writhing in pain. You scream in horror as your feet and hands blister, and your hair catches fire. You gnaw at your tongue, trying desperately to relieve the torment and your throat becomes raw from all your screaming.

You go under the surface of molten lava gnashing your teeth. As you gasp for air the burning brimstone flows into your mouth. You are on fire inside and out. You try to focus your eyes in the endless, everlasting, permanent dwelling place of total torment but they burn with such pain as though they were melting in the sockets.

Through the smoke and flame, you finally focus on the worms that have begun to totally engulf your body. They are crawling all over you, and you realize in horror that they are feasting on you. You can feel them as they crawl in and out of you, but you are not consumed.

The horrid smell of blazing sulfur combined with the sickening odor of burning hair and scorching flesh linger in your nose and nausea overwhelms you. The roar of the flames and the piercing screams of the damned seem to tear at your eardrums. Oh, for just a moment of silence! But that silence never comes. You can't run away this time.

Your thoughts return to the time you were in a Bible-believing, preaching Church. You can still remember the time when the preacher was talking to you about this hopeless place of darkness and pain, but you didn't want to listen. For eternity you will scream those words again and again, over and over, but alas, they are not heard.

This isn't fantasy or imagination. No, this is reality, and your reality without Christ in hell."

Now that doesn't seem to be a very fun body to have; I mean who in their right mind would want to have a body like that, especially when they didn't have to. But that's what we deserve for sinning against the Holy and Righteous God. We're His enemies and are ungodly; we rebelled just like the devil and his demons. Forever and ever, we deserve what I just described. But God's merciful love kicked in and He did something about it. He sent "agapao" (a verb, it's an action) His Son, not because we were worthy; it's a self-sacrificial action, purely for the benefit of another person, us. "I'm going to save you from that place. I'm doing all the work." You don't maintain it, you don't earn it, you don't try to keep it. It's all complete. All you have to do is just say, "Yes, that's what I want."

Again, He will give you the exact opposite. **John 3:16:** perish versus eternal life. He flips it around. So, you go from deserving a body of pain and you go to a body of perfection.

I Corinthians 15:42,44: "It is the same way for the resurrection of the dead. Our earthly bodies, which die and decay, will be different when they are resurrected, for they will never die. They are natural human bodies now, but when they are raised, they will be spiritual bodies. For just as there are natural bodies, so also there are spiritual bodies."

The Bible says that when we die as a born-again Christian, we said yes to God's merciful love through His Son, Jesus Christ, His merciful acts, self-sacrificial action, His death on the cross, I won't get that body of pain, I'm going to get a brand-new resurrected body. When you take a look at the characteristics of that, it means your body's never going to die, it's never going to rot, it's never going to decay, break down or age. And that means there will be no more back aches, no more broken bones, no more disease, and yes ladies, no more anti-aging creams. Our new bodies will never wear down and they'll never wear out.

"One day there was this 85-year-old couple who had been married for almost 60 years, and suddenly they both died in a car crash. And they had been in good health for the last ten years mainly due to her interest in healthy food, and exercise.

Well, when they reached the pearly gates, St. Peter took them to their mansion which was decked out with a beautiful kitchen and master bath suite and Jacuzzi.

And they 'oohed and aahed' but the old man asked Peter how much all this was going to cost. 'It's free,' Peter replied, 'this is Heaven.'

So next they go out back to survey the championship golf course that the home was backed up to. And they learned they would have golfing privileges every day, and each week the course would change to a new one representing one of the great golf courses back on earth.

And so, the old man asked, 'What are the green fees?' And Peter replied, 'This is Heaven, you play for free.'

Well next they went to the clubhouse and saw the lavish buffet lunch with all the cuisines of the world laid right out before them.

And so the old man asked, 'Well, how much to eat?' And Peter by now is getting a little exasperated and he says, 'Don't you get it yet? This is Heaven, it's free!' So, the old man asked timidly, 'Well, where are all the low fat and low cholesterol tables?'

And Peter exclaimed, 'Well hello, that's the best part...you can eat as much as you like of whatever you like, and you never get fat, and you never get sick. This is Heaven.'

Well, with that the old man went into a fit of anger, throwing down his hat and stomping on it, and shrieking wildly. And so, Peter and his wife were both trying to calm him down and they asked him what was wrong.

And the old man looked at his wife and said, 'This is all your fault. If it weren't for your stupid prunes and bran muffins, I could have been here ten years ago!'"

Then as if that wasn't cool enough, our new bodies will not only be imperishable, but they'll be spiritual. That means that our body will be just like Jesus' body after He was raised from the dead. And if you study the characteristics of Jesus' resurrected body you see that He was not affected by matter. He could walk through doors. He could travel instantly anywhere at any time. And that means in heaven, there'll be no traffic, no toll booths and no more car taxes, praise God! And folks, I don't know about you, but that's not a very hard choice to make here. I'd much rather have a body of perfection than a body of pain, how about you? And to think that it's not only free for the asking, but we don't deserve it! Now that's what I call love!

A.W Tozer said, *"The vague and tenuous hope that God is too kind to punish the ungodly has become a deadly opiate for the consciences of millions."*

People aren't convicted of sin because the new version of God's love, even in the churches, is He doesn't care about sin, He's just love, love, love. And if you never respond to the Biblical gospel, you just shook their hand with a false gospel straight into hell. And you are going to stand accountable to God for that.

The 3rd way the Bible reveals the merciful Love of God is that God gives His enemies a Heavenly Greeting instead of hellish goodbye. Let's draw one more aspect. What were we prior to getting saved through Jesus Christ?

Romans 5:8 "But God demonstrates his own love for us in this: While we were still sinners, Christ died for us."

Now we have a couple of different things. It says that Jesus went to the cross because we were the saintly ones, we were the super-duper spiritual ones. No! Let's add them all together. Apart from Christ, under the wrath of God, having sinned against a righteous and Holy God, every day you lived prior to coming to Christ you are looked upon as an enemy of God, ungodly, and a sinner. So, in that state, God sent His Son, as a self-sacrificial action, purely for the benefit of all of us. He sent Jesus to live the life we could never live, to die on the cross, take our punishment, our place, and all you have to do is receive that. You say, "No!" As an enemy, ungodly, sinner, what do you get? You get justice. It won't be social justice. It'll be Biblical justice. You're going to get a hellish goodbye. Sometimes people, right before they die, it's not good. Here are a few quotes:

NON-CHRISTIAN DYING WORDS

Voltaire: *"I am abandoned by God and Man! I shall go to Hell! O' Jesus Christ."*

David Hume: The atheist died in utter despair with an awful scene crying out, *"I am in the flames!"*

Karl Marx: Was on his deathbed surrounded by candles burning to lucifer and screamed at his nurse who asked him if he had any last words. *"Go on, get out! Last words are for fools who haven't said enough."*

Thomas Payne: *"I would give worlds, if I had them, if the Age of Reason had never been published. O Lord, help me! Christ, help me! Stay with me! It is hell to be left alone!"*

Nietzsche: Who said, *"God is Dead"* died insane, completely out of his mind.

Sir Thomas Scott: *"Until now I thought there was no God or hell. Now I know there is both, and I am doomed."*

Sir Francis Newport: *"Do not tell me there is no God for I know there is one, and that I am in His angry presence! You need not tell me there is no hell, for I already feel my soul slipping into its fires! I know that I am lost forever."*

Apart from Christ, you wanted justice, you've got justice. You spurned the Biblical, merciful, love of God. God gave you what you demanded, justice. Well, you got it. You went there. To hell. And you started getting a taste of it before you left this earth.

I'll give you one more story a pastor shared from Texas. He witnessed to a guy working on the oil rigs. He was a big guy and a skeptic. He didn't need Jesus. The pastor witnessed to him for a long time. He just didn't want anything to do with Jesus. Then the preacher got a call that a pile of pipes, oil rigging pipes, fell on this guy. They crushed his chest. They rushed him to the hospital. The pastor was told that he wasn't going to make it. This pastor wanted to share the gospel with this guy one more time. He's rounding the corner getting to his room and he could hear the guy screaming in pain. The pastor just gets to his room, and he sees that the guy had torn up the mattress, he's grabbing, clawing on it and then he cried, "Preacher." Then he died, going down. Why would you choose to leave that way when it didn't have to be that way? And it's irreversible. You can't change it, it's done. Or you could respond to God's merciful love of God, the true gospel and you get the polar opposite. You don't need to leave that way; you get to leave this way:

CHRISTIAN'S LAST WORDS

The famous Christian, Dwight Moody awoke from sleep shortly before he died said: *"Earth recedes. Heaven opens before me. If this is death, it is sweet! There is no valley here. God is calling me, and I must go."*

And Moody's son said, *"No, no, Father. You're dreaming."* And Moody replied, *"I am not dreaming. I have seen within the gates. This is my triumph; this is my coronation day! It is glorious!"*

Augustus Toplady, preacher and author of the hymn, "Rock of Ages": *"The consolations of God to such an unworthy wretch are so abundant that He leaves me nothing to pray for but a continuance of them. I enjoy Heaven already in my soul."*

Lady Glenorchy: *"If this is dying, it is the pleasantest thing imaginable."*

John Pawson, minister: *"I know I am dying, but my deathbed is a bed of roses. I have no thorns planted upon my pillow. In Christ, Heaven is already begun!"*

John A. Lyth: *"Can this be death? Why, it is better than living! Tell them I die happy in Jesus!"*

Adoniram Judson, American missionary to Burma: *"I go with the gladness of a boy bounding away from school. I feel so strong in Christ."*

Martha McCrackin: *"How bright the room! How full of angels!"*

Mary Frances: *"Oh, that I could tell you what joy I possess! The Lord does shine with such power upon my soul!"*

Sir David Brewster, scientist and inventor of the kaleidoscope: *"I will see Jesus; I shall see Him as He is! I have had the light for many years. Oh, how bright it is! I feel so safe and satisfied!"*

A Moslem woman, whose child had died at 16 years of age asked a Christian missionary, *"What did you do to our daughter?"* The missionary replied, *"We did nothing."*

But the mother persisted, *"Oh, yes, you did! She died smiling. Our people do not die like that."* As it turned out, the girl had found Christ and believed on Him only a few months before. Fear of death had gone, and hope and joy had taken its place.

And finally, a Chinese communist, through whom many Christians had been executed, said to a Pastor: *"I have seen many of you die. The Christians die in a different way. What is your secret?"*

I'll tell you what the secret is. We Christians die in Christ. We've received the merciful love of God through Him, and we're headed to Heaven! And that's why it's not a very hard choice to make here. I'd much rather have a heavenly greeting than a hellish goodbye, how about you? And to think that it's not only free for the asking, but we don't deserve it! Now that's what I call love! And it's the same conclusion this guy makes.

Another quick story about a lady I pastored in Northern California. She was dying from the flesh-eating disease. If you know anything about that, that is probably one of the most painful ways to go. Eating her body alive. She spent the last day and a half in the hospital. Every time anybody came into the room, nurses, doctors, didn't matter who it was, she would literally interrupt them and say, "Can't you hear the angels? Can't you hear them sing?" She was in a whole other world. It wasn't just the morphine. I believe that God was giving her a taste of where she was headed. Why? Because of the beautiful, wonderful, merciful "agapao" love of God. Isn't that awesome? When you understand Biblical love, it's hard to keep your mouth shut.

John MacArthur: *"The particular love of God for His own is overwhelming. It is powerful. If you don't stand in awe of it, then you don't really grasp its significance. We ought to be in awe, and like Israel, humiliated before such love. He does not owe it to us. Yet He condescends to love us, nonetheless. If our hearts aren't stirred with love for God in return, then there's something terribly wrong with us."*

Maybe we are infected ourselves with this unbiblical view of God's love. If you can't seem to appreciate the fact that through Jesus Christ, God will give His enemies a palace in Heaven instead of a pit in hell, a body of perfection instead of a body of pain, and a Heavenly greeting instead of a hellish goodbye, then something is terribly wrong with you! If we had any idea of the depths of God's love, we would not only fall on our knees in reverence and kiss the very feet of Christ, but we'd get up on our feet and run to tell everyone immediately of their need of Christ!

That's Biblical love. Do you see how twisted it has become? You just got to love everybody, whatever lifestyle. Don't talk about sin, don't talk about it because God's love, God's love, God's love. It's sick and it's unbiblical. It's destroying lives, its destroying churches, its destroying our country, and dare I say, that's not the gospel.

People say, "Yeah, Yeah, I appreciate God's merciful love and I'm glad that I won't go to hell, I'm not going to get that body of pain. I'm looking forward to that transition from this world into Heaven. It's going to be awesome. And yeah, I should be telling other people about it." How can you truly understand the love of God if you don't understand the justice of God? What we deserve. How can people appreciate what Christ did for them on the cross and His death if you don't ever mention sin. And it isn't just sin, the penalty of sin is death, and we deserve to perish and go to hell. Why are we so ashamed of that? This is the Christianese that oftentimes goes around in churches because you get kind of guilty. I should tell other people about the good news of Jesus, God's merciful love.

There's a second horrible trend in the American Church, and that is this: one half of the American Church not only denies the existence of hell, but the other half tries to soften the existence of hell. For instance, the 1st phrase people come up with to try to soften the existence of a hell is, "Hey man, you don't want to have a Christless Eternity, do you?" Excuse me? What in the world is a "Christless Eternity?" What does a "Christless Eternity" mean to a person who doesn't know Christ? In fact, this is their problem. They already don't know Christ and they think they're fine. So how does the phrase "Christless Eternity" help them realize that unless they get right with Jesus Christ that they're going to hell? And they need to receive Christ as their savior to be rescued from that.

Answer? It's not! It's actually hurting them, not helping them! They already don't know Christ and they think they are okay. Christ means nothing, there is no sting and there should be conviction. When you are really giving out the gospel, they should go, "I'm in a bad relationship with God because of my sin." Then you tell them about His love and what He's done through Christ.

The 2nd phrase people come up with to try to soften the existence of a hell is, "Hey, don't you want to go to heaven?" Well, duuuuh! Excuse me? Of course, people want to go to heaven! Who in the world does not want to go to heaven? And again, this is precisely their problem. Most people already think that they're going to heaven… Yet the Bible says without Jesus Christ you're not going to heaven, you're going to hell! It's not just that you're not going to heaven, it's please don't go to hell!

The 3rd phrase people come up with to try to soften the existence of a hell is, "Hey man, you need to get saved." And I must admit, that's a little bit better, but saved from what? If you listen to the false gospel of social justice, it's saved from a poor economic existence. It's saved from a low self-esteem. It's saved from what? A bad life? A mediocre existence. A chicken dinner? A zit, a pimple? What? Saved from what? Don't assume people know what you're talking about because guess what? They don't! And again, this is their problem. You need to spell it out and say, "You need to get saved alright, you need to get saved from hell! Jesus Christ died on the cross to save you from hell." I didn't say that. Jesus did! Why is it so wrong? Why can't we ever say it? It's supposed to sting. Hell is supposed to be scary. That's why Jesus talked about it so much. Because He is love and He demonstrated that love so that we wouldn't have to go there, but we never talk about it. How can you appreciate what He's done if you don't understand what we deserve? That's your gospel? You need to get saved. Saved from what?

The 4th phrase people come up with to try to soften the existence of a hell is, "Hey man listen, I don't want to scare them off" with all this hell talk. Excuse me? Think about it. Where are you going to scare them off too? Hell #2? What in the world is the option here? There isn't! You're either going straight to heaven or you're going straight to hell. The cross of Christ is the only way out of that predicament. And everybody that takes a breath of life and if they have not responded to God's merciful love, you're headed there. And they need to know that. And you know what that does? That gets rid of procrastination. You probably have heard, "Well, I'm kind of young, maybe when I get older, and I've done the things in life that I want to do." You could die right now and go straight to where? Hell. "Maybe I'll make it my next New Year's Resolution, you know what I'm saying?" You could die right now and go to hell. Why are we so ashamed of a Biblical word that defines and magnifies God's love through Jesus? Do you see how twisted even that has become?

So, here is the Biblical way to share the GOOD NEWS of the GOSPEL to those around us in light of BIBLICAL LOVE.

Ron Reagan: *"Don't go to hell. Please I beg of you. Don't go to hell."*

Narrator: *"Mr. Ron Reagan also experienced visions of hell while clinically dead."*

Ron Reagan: *"If you don't get to a hospital, you'll bleed to death in just a few minutes. A young paramedic looked down into my face and I could barely see him. I was so weak. He said, 'Sir, you need Jesus Christ.' And as he was talking to me, it appeared like the ambulance literally exploded in flames. I thought it had actually blown up. It was filled with smoke and immediately I was moving through that smoke as if through a tunnel and after some period of time, coming out of the smoke and out of the darkness, I began to hear the voices of a multitude of people screaming and groaning and crying.*

As I looked down, the sensation was looking down upon a volcanic opening. Seeing fire and smoke and people inside of this burning place, screaming and crying. They were burning but they weren't burning up. They weren't being consumed. And then the sensation of moving downward into this, but the most terrible part of it, I began to recognize many of the people that I was seeing in these flames. It was as if a close-up lens on a camera was bringing their faces close to me. I could see their features and see the agony and the pain and the frustration. A number of them began to call my name and said Ronnie don't come to this place. There's no way out. There's no escape if you come here. There's no way out.

I believe the most painful part of it was the loneliness. And the depression was so heavy that there was no hope. There was no escape. There was no way out of this place. The smell was like sulfur, like an electric welder. And as I am looking into this pit, this place of fire and screams and torment, I just fade out into blackness. When I opened my eyes, I'm in a hospital room in Knoxville, Tennessee. My wife is sitting by. I didn't know the sinner's prayer. I didn't know the Roman Road to salvation. But my prayer was this, 'God, if you exist and Jesus, if You are God's lamb, please, please kill me or cure me.' And Jesus Christ became Lord and Savior of my life that morning. From that moment I knew that I had to tell the story of what had happened to me. My life was only spared to tell others about the place that I had seen and the hope of Jesus Christ to save mankind from this terrible fate."

People in hell wish that people on earth would tell their family to not go to hell. Did you know I just quoted **Luke 16**? What did the guy say from hell? Warn my family not to come to this place. They know it's real but it's too late. You want justice? Don't ask for justice. You should celebrate the merciful love of God, that He doesn't give us what we deserve through Jesus Christ. When you understand that and appreciate it every day, you know what it does? It makes you want to evangelize.

For 29 years I have been saved. I'm not saying that to boast, don't misunderstand me. Every day for 29 years I have been praying for my family and several of them have gotten saved. You know why it keeps me on track to do that? Because I know what I deserve as a former occultist, satanist, new ager, scoffer and mocker. I certainly was an enemy; ungodly sinner and I know what I deserve. I'm so thankful for God's merciful love for me. I know what I deserve, and I don't want my family to go there.

I still have family that are scoffing and mocking, like I used to do and so do you. If we really understand true Biblical love, we don't waste time. I don't care if they rejected Christ 100 million times. My mom did for 28 years but praise God, the next time she said yes. Don't quit. It's not just something that we have to do. If you love Him, you keep His commands and share the good news, the great commission is the most loving thing we could do, that's why it's called the gospel. Good News. "Let me tell you about Biblical love." Paul said, "I'm not afraid of the gospel." You keep on sharing, you keep on praying, and you never quit. If they are still breathing, you keep sharing.

God's love is multi-faceted. It's like a diamond. It's one diamond but it has many different sides to it. If you want to get the whole picture, then you have to deal with all the facets. When the Scripture says, God is love; He is love itself, He is perfect love. To get the full understanding of what that means, you have to look at all the facets.

The next way God demonstrates that He is love, is by giving us compassion. And we see that in the Prodigal Son story. But what we are going to focus on isn't just the son, but it's the reaction of the father. We understand what is going on culturally and what this son said to his dad, it's amazing, the reaction of the dad. It brings out another facet of God's love, i.e., compassion that He throws on us.

Luke 15:11-24: "Jesus continued, 'There was a man who had two sons. The younger one said to his father, 'Father, give me my share of the estate.' So, he divided his property between them. Not long after that, the younger son got together all he had, set off for a distant country and there squandered his wealth in wild living. After he had spent everything, there was a severe famine in that whole country, and he began to be in need. So, he went and hired himself out to a citizen of that country, who sent him to his fields to feed pigs. He longed to fill his stomach with the pods that the pigs were eating, but no one gave him anything. When he came to his senses, he said 'How many of my father's hired men have food to spare, and here I am starving to death! I will set out and go back to my father and say to him: Father, I have sinned against Heaven and against you. I am no longer worthy to be called your son; make me like one of your hired men.' So, he got up and went to his father. But while he was still a long way off, his father saw him and was filled with compassion for him; he ran to his son, threw his arms around him and kissed him.'"

Now what did that say? He was a long way off, but his dad was looking for him. He forgot what he did, and the dad was looking for him. And he was a long way off and he started taking action. He showed compassion.

Luke 15:11-24, cont.: The son said to him, 'Father, I have sinned against Heaven and against you. I am no longer worthy to be called your son.' But the father said to his servants, 'Quick! Bring the best robe and put it on him. Put a ring on his finger and sandals on his feet. Bring the fattened calf and kill it. Let's have a feast and celebrate. For this son of mine was dead and is alive again, he was lost and is found.' So, they began to celebrate.'"

Again, this is the prodigal son story, and I'm sure you're familiar with it. But what you've got to understand is that it's not just a story about the son's need of forgiveness but of a father's incredible compassion. You see, the word "compassion" comes from the Greek word "splanchna." It literally means "to be moved in one's innards or bowels." It was the metaphor of that day to speak of the seat of affection or emotions. For instance, today, we would say we are moved in our heart for someone. But back then they would say they were moved in their bowels for someone.

"Splanchna" or "compassion" wasn't just an emotional feeling. But get this…it was "a loving action generated out of pity." And this is exactly what we see with this father. Out of pity he refrained from giving his son what he really deserved, right? I mean, stop and think about it. If your son basically told you to hurry up and die so I can have my inheritance, and that's what's going on here, and then he went off and blew the whole thing in sinful living and came back, what would you do? You wouldn't give him the fatted calf. Are you kidding? You'd give him the fatted casket, right? The fabulous kick in the pants! But not this father! No! What'd he do? He showed compassion for his son! And not by just having pity for him, but he threw a party for him! Can you believe that? Is that love or what?

Now that is an example of God's love. God has compassion on us. He looks upon us in our sinfulness. We squandered it all away in sinful living and rottenness, and we spurned Him away. We wanted nothing to do with him, just doing our own things. We are here covered in depravity and sinfulness, and God, out of compassion and pity on us, He says, "I'm going to throw you a party." And we, as born-again Christians, are headed to that party. The Marriage Supper of the Lamb. It's going to be awesome.

But herein lies our problem. We live in a society that no longer pleads for the compassion of God. People today no longer think they're pitiful. No! They think they're wonderful. They don't think they need pity from God. They think they're owed a party from God! But as we saw, if we got what was owed to us, what would we get? A pit in hell, a body of pain, and a hellish goodbye, right? And I don't know about you, I'd rather have pity than that kind of party! So, let's take a closer look at this compassion of God, so we can better understand true Biblical love from God.

The 1st way the Bible reveals the compassionate love of God is that He died for those who wanted Him dead. I hope that what Christ did on the cross for you never gets old. It is one of the greatest acts of compassion.

Luke 23:32-34: "Two others, both criminals, were led out to be executed with him. Finally, they came to a place called The Skull. All three were crucified there – Jesus on the center cross, and the two criminals on either side. Jesus said, 'Father, forgive these people, because they don't know what they are doing.'"

So, here we see Jesus was not only killed on the cross between two criminals, but He was put there because people considered Him one. Can you imagine the sinfulness of that? I mean, here we have God Himself, coming to the earth to save the lost, but they rejected Him, they rejected His teachings, accused Him, and beat Him, and mocked Him, and spit at Him, and flogged Him, and now you put Him on the cross! Can you believe that? This is God in the flesh. Put between two criminals. He's never done anything wrong. Talk about sin! And what did He say? "Forgive them for they know not what they do."

Sometimes it makes me sick to see Hollywood wearing the cross. The occult wears the cross, but it's upside down. They have to have on a cross that is about three feet long, made of gold, to show they're a

Christian. But what really gets me is the lost don't know any better. They say they are Christian, but then they are singing their songs about immorality and things of that nature, but people can see the cross. Believe it or not, the American Church has committed an even bigger sin than that! How? By becoming numb to this amazing act of the love of God.

It appears to me that we have long forgotten the true meaning of the cross! For your information, the cross is not just a Christian religious symbol to hang around your neck! It was a horrible instrument of suffering and death! The cross was the firing squad, the hangman's noose, the gas chamber of our day. It was the means of which to execute the worst of criminals. Yet Jesus was not a criminal! He was the Christ, the Messiah, the Savior of the world. He who knew no sin voluntarily allowed himself to die to take away our sins. Today, when one is executed it's fast, it's over. You get the needle, you get the gas, it's over. But not the cross. If you forgot what He went through, let's take a look at the cross of Christ to see just a little bit of what He went through for you and me.

Speaker #1: *"Jesus has endured hours of misery. But the worst of the ordeal is yet to come."*

Speaker #2: *"The nails that they used, and we have many of them excavated here and there. They were usually quite long, they have a very large head, the shank is square and cross-sectioned or forged, they are* 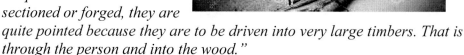 *quite pointed because they are to be driven into very large timbers. That is through the person and into the wood."*

Speaker #1: *"In quick succession the nails are pounded into his feet and hands."*

Speaker #3: *"There are many cases, in which for example, an injury to the hand from a bullet or even a knife, would cause what is called causalgia. Initially the pain itself is just where the injury is."*

Speaker #4: *"If the median nerve is ruptured or injured, will also cause severe, excruciating, burning like pain, like lightning bolts traversing the arm to the spinal cord. Now we know from experiences, during the war, especially WWII, where there was a condition called causalgia, which is a condition caused by injury to the median nerve. The pain was so terrific that even morphine wouldn't help, and they had to actually operate on the spinal column in order to decrease or eliminate that sort of pain."*

Speaker #3: *"It is so severe, that if you blow on the skin of the hand where the pain is, the patient would scream, abnormally."*

Speaker #4: *"When a nail pierces the top of the foot, goes through the top of the foot, whether it went through each foot separately or both feet it would rupture or at least injure the plantar nerves which would go down between each of the bones. The pain would be very similar to the pain of the hand because causalgia is the same medical condition. It would cause a severe lightning bolt like pain right up the leg, burning, searing, type pains."*

And you're just getting started. Who is this? This is Jesus Christ, this is God in the flesh, **Philippians 2**, He took on the form of a servant, became obedient, to die like that for us, and it had nothing to do with Him. And why would He do something like that? Because God is love. God has shown "splanchna," compassion upon us. He looked down upon us and took pity in our messed-up state. He said, "You know what? I'll let you guys treat me like a criminal and put me on that cross. I'll do that for the joy set before me, because one day I'll be able to throw you a party." He took away all our sins.

THE MEDICAL DESCRIPTION OF THE CROSS

As Jesus slowly sags down with more weight on the nails in the wrists, excruciating fiery pain shoots through His fingers and up the arms to explode in the brain. The nails in the wrists are putting pressure on the median nerves.

Therefore, as He pushes Himself upward to avoid this stretching torment, He places the full weight on the nail through His feet. But this causes a searing agony as the nail tears through the nerves between the bones of His feet.

Then His arms get fatigued, cramps sweep through His muscles, knotting them in deep, relentless, throbbing pain. And with these cramps come the inability to push Himself upward to breathe. Air can be drawn into the lungs, but not exhaled.

So, Jesus fights to raise Himself in order to get even one small breath. In spasms, He's able to push Himself upward to exhale and get more oxygen but each time its less and less.

He experiences hours of horrible pain, as the tissue is torn from His lacerated back trying to move up and down against the rough timber just so He can breathe. But then another agony arrives. A deep crushing pain in the chest begins as the area around His heart slowly fills with serum and begins to compress His heart.

It's almost over. The loss of fluids has reached a critical level. The heart is struggling to pump blood, as the tortured lungs make a frantic effort to gasp small gulps of air.

He can feel the chill of death creeping through His tissues. And finally, Jesus can allow His body to die, but not before saying this, "Father, forgive them! For they know not what they do!"

I don't know about you, but that doesn't seem to be a very fun way to die, how about you? I mean, who in their right mind would volunteer to die like that, especially for people who wanted you dead! But that's exactly what Jesus did! Talk about the love of God!

We're just getting started with just a little facet of the Biblical definition that God is love. Now what I just stated is Biblical, and then go back to what those guys are saying in the church. Their version of God is love is, you can be a homosexual; any kind of perversion can go and if you say anything, you're a bigot. That's not just gross and blasphemous, but do you see how that cheapens the real love of God? When you understand the love of God you can't keep your mouth shut. It's crazy.

Oswald Chambers: *"All Heaven is interested in the cross of Christ, all hell is terribly afraid of it, while men are the only beings who more or less ignore its meaning."*

When you understand the cross of Christ, and what He did, you're going to say, "Thank you God for showing compassion upon me. Not giving me what I deserve." And then he does something else.

The 2nd way the Bible reveals the Compassionate Love of God is that He Continually Forgives Our Continual Sins.

Hebrews 7:24-25: "But because Jesus lives forever, He has a permanent priesthood. Therefore, He is able to save completely those who come to God through Him, because He always lives to intercede for them."

So here we see Jesus not only died on the cross to forgive us of our sins, but He always lives to intercede for our sins. And do you have any idea of the significance of that statement? The One who died for those who wanted Him dead not only forgives them once, but again and again! Isn't that incredible?

I mean, let's put it in its context. For instance, let's go back to the prodigal son story. There we saw how that father demonstrated an amazing amount of compassion to his son, right? He didn't give him what he deserved. He gave him a party, right? But now imagine that after the party and they ate the fatted calf, the son went off the next month and did it again. And then he went out the next week and did it again. And then he went out the next day and did it again! And he kept on doing it! I mean, come on! If most of us were that father we'd be tempted to say, "Okay pal, this is the fourth time I've killed the fatted calf this week. Hello! What's your problem here?! Cows don't grow on trees!" Right? But believe it or not, this is exactly what God does for you and I every single day. And He never runs out of cows!

Even after we get saved, even after we come back to the Father as Christians, we still sin. How many sin as Christians? But what does God do? "You've reached this point, and this is it. You had that party, and you should have known better. You should have walked straight from that point. I'm done!" No. He does it again. He does it again. He does it again. God does it for you and I, and He never runs out of cows! Because Jesus is always interceding on our behalf! All of our sins are gone forevermore, poof! They've just…disappeared, like some sort of Divine Miracle, like this guy experienced.

Husband: *"Did you say you were going to make dinner? I don't remember."*

Wife: *"What? I just wish you would take some initiative and cook your own dinner for once. I've been at work too, you know, and now I get to come home and pack the dishwasher and unpack the dishwasher, cook dinner, and you know what? I just can't live like this."*

Husband: *"Hey, Hey, Hey, relax, it's going to be alright."*

Wife: *"How?"*

Husband: *"Come here, I want to show you. I've been doing this. See this basket. I don't know how it's doing this, if it's the house or what. But any dirty clothes you put in this basket, somehow the next day it's clean, folded and in a perfect pile on the bed."*

Wife: *"You're not serious."*

Husband: *"I couldn't believe it either, but it just keeps happening. That's why I didn't want to tell you. I didn't want to jinx it."*

Wife: *"You are insane."*

Husband: *"Try it. Go ahead and try it, unless it has only chosen me."*

Wife: *"I can't do this."*

Husband: *"Wait. There are other things too. Plates, cutlery, pizza boxes, dirty tissues, anything you leave on this coffee table, just vanishes overnight. Sometimes I will stay up at night to see this thing, but sure enough the next day it's all gone. It just left. It vanished, it's magic."*

The next morning the husband is talking to two police officers:

Husband: *"She wouldn't have just left me. It just happened. I heard her get up in the middle of the night. She must have fallen onto the coffee table and just vanished."*

Female cop: *"Are you insane?"*

Male cop: *"No, he's not insane, I've got the same coffee table at home."*

Now how many of you guys would say that guy's never going to get his wife back after that one, huh? Talk about living in a dream world! The clothes magically wash themselves; the dirty dishes magically disappear! Wow! Now, here's what's wild. That might be make believe for that guy and his wife…but not with God. He really does magically wash us clean! He really does cleanse us from all our dirty sins…poof…it's gone! I didn't say that. He did!

Micah 7:18,19: "Who is a God like you, Who pardons sin and forgives the transgression. You will again have compassion on us; You will tread our sins underfoot and hurl all our iniquities into the depths of the sea."

Isaiah 43:25: "I, even I, am He Who blots out your transgressions, for My own sake, and remembers your sins no more."

Hebrews 8:12: "For I will forgive their wickedness and will remember their sins no more."

Poof! It's gone! Just like that magic coffee table! Isn't that awesome! God remembers them no more, they are gone! Have you ever hit that delete button on your computer? Where did that letter go? It just disappeared. It's gone just like Jesus always intercedes for us. You sin, delete, you sin, delete, you sin, delete. In fact, the Bible goes on to say that Jesus not only died to save us from our sins, and erase our sins, but get this. He died for us so we can be presented to the Father as if we had never sinned! Is that a mind blower or what? It's an amazing kind of love, you know what I mean. Why? Because stop and think about it. Who in their right mind would not only forgive those who wanted you dead, but get this, keep on forgiving them again and again. I will take that love, "agapao" over their love "eros" any day. When you understand true Biblical love. WOW! Here is a true modern day prodigal son story.

"This happened to a father in Salinas, California. He too had two sons, and one was highly respected in the community, very subservient to his father, while the other had a bit of a rebellious streak in him.

From an early age, this younger brother decided that as soon as he turned 18 that he would make his dad live up to his promise. He promised that as soon as his sons turned 18, if they wanted, he would cash out, basically divide the land and the property and inheritance, and give it to them.

So sure enough, the younger son, when he turned 18, he told his dad that he wanted his money, give him his inheritance.

But his dad pleaded with him because he saw the immaturity in his son, and said, 'Now is not the time. Please, just hang with me three more years…four more years. Let me prepare you to develop some more maturity, and then it's yours.'

The son said, 'No. A promise is a promise. You said 18. I want it now!'

So reluctantly, his dad made good on the promise, wrote the check, and the son cashed it in, in an amount for what would be, literally, today, millions of dollars.

So, he did what any freshman would do at 18. He took the money, and he said, 'I'm going to get as far away from here and as far away from my dad's rules as I possibly can,' he jumped on a train, and he went to New York City.

As soon as he got to New York, he started taking his money and just throwing it away. He grabbed him the nicest sports car he could get. He grabbed some buddies and got an elite penthouse on the top of one of the high-rises.

Then he began buying every kind of dating relationship money could buy.

Eventually, this led to some alcohol problems, gambling problems, and before long, he began to spend more money and actually accrue more debt than he could to pay off, which meant eventually the creditors came after him.

So, then he had to move out of the penthouse. He had to let go of his sports car, and before he knew it, he was on the Upper East Side of New York wandering the streets.

Then, his alcoholism had gotten to the point that he was literally pilfering through garbage cans trying to find bottles that had remnants of alcohol so he could try to get a drink.

Then, the STD's he'd picked up from loose living, now covered his body
in sores all over, and all of his friends had left him, until one day he was
on the street, and he came to a reality check. He came to his senses.

'If I don't do something about this now, I'm going to die out here.'

So, he managed to bum some money off of a couple of his old friends to
buy a train ticket back to Salinas and his thought was, 'If I can only get
back to my dad, then I can just start over.'

So, he takes the train ride. A couple of days pass, and he finally winds up
in Salinas, gets off the train, walks into the square, and he realizes, 'Wait a
minute. There is no way I can see my dad face-to-face. There's no way
he's going to accept me back after what I did. He's just going to say I told
you so.'

So, he goes into a café and begins to weep and think about what he was
going to do, and then he decided to write a letter to his dad. When he
finished, he went out into the streets and found one of his dad's farm
workers, gave him the letter, and said, 'Will you take this to my dad
because I can't bear to see him right now?'

The farm worker did and here's an actual copy of the letter.

He said, 'Father, I realize what I've done. I've wasted not only your
money but my life, which was important to you. I can't even begin to tell
you about the awful things that I've done.

I'm embarrassed. I'm at the end of my rope. I know nothing else to do but
ask you if I can return home. I know that there's no reason why you
should accept me back, but I plead, and I beg with you that if you would,
even as a farm worker on your land, accept me back, I'll do anything for
no pay. Just for the room and board.'

He said, 'Father, I have just enough money to take the train that passes by
our ranch in front of the apple orchard near the edge of the property. I'm

going by there on the train tomorrow at 1:00 p.m., and if you would accept me back…

I would ask that you simply drape an old sheet over one of the trees nearest the railroad, and as I'm passing by, I'll see the signal, and I'll know you've accepted me to come home.

If that sheet is not there, then I won't stop at the train station. I'll just keep going. I can't bear to see you face-to-face. I don't have the courage. I've done too much, and I have no idea what's going to happen with the rest of my life. Your son.'

Imagine being in that position. A whole sleepless night went by filled with anxiety for this young man. The next morning, he jumped on the train.

As soon as he got to the train, he walked to the very back of the train, and he sat down next to this old man, and he just put his face in his hands and just began to weep as he contemplated what he may or may not see.

He began to share with the old man his story about the things he had done and how he was coming back. Soon enough, as the train passed outside of Salinas and got to the outside edge of the town around where their ranch was.

He looked to the old man, and he said, 'Can you do me favor? Can you just go to the window, and just tell me if you see one sheet anywhere in this apple orchard? I can't bear to look.'

And so, the old man jumped up. He went to the window, and he looked out. Then he looked back at the young man, and he said, 'I think you need to come see this for yourself.'

When he jumped up, he went to the window, and he looked out, and behold, as far as his eye could see for five square miles, there was a sheet on every tree."

Come home son…

The Bible says that God has loved us with an everlasting love, a compassionate love. God says, "You want to know how much I love you? Is the sun not enough? Is the moon not enough? Are the food and shelter you have not enough? Is the air you breathe not enough? Then how about this? How about I actually send My own Son to die in your place so you can be with Me forever? So, you can be with Me forever." That's compassion.

But there's one missing element. It wasn't for His own son that you'd expect to have a Fatherly compassion for. It wasn't for wonderful people who were nice and kind to Him. But it was for you and I who hated His guts, nailed Him on a cross and who even after being saved, have the audacity to keep on sinning again, and again, and again! And He says, "I'm going to have compassion on you. I'm going to show pity. I'm not going to give you what you deserve. I'm going to delete, delete, delete."

Isn't that amazing. I'll take that any day of the week over "eros." You can be a tree, a flea, or identify as a cat. And then that's the message of love that the world is hearing from the church.

The 3rd way God reveals that He is Love is by Giving Us Kindness. Have you heard that in the Scripture?

Titus 3:1-7: "Remind the people to be subject to rulers and authorities, to be obedient, to be ready to do whatever is good to slander no one, to be peaceable and considerate, and to show true humility toward all men. At one time we too were foolish, disobedient, deceived and enslaved by all kinds of passions and pleasures. We lived in malice and envy, being hated and hating one another. But when the kindness and love of God our Savior appeared, He saved us, not because of righteous things we had done, but because of His mercy. He saved us through the washing of rebirth and renewal by the Holy Spirit, whom He poured out on us generously through Jesus Christ our Savior, so that, having been justified by His grace, we might become heirs having the hope of eternal life."

Now, according to our text, you can't get any plainer than this. The Bible clearly says that nobody is getting to heaven because they're so wonderful. Are you kidding?! What did the text say? At one time we too were disobedient fools, enslaved to sin, and full of hatred, right? That means you aren't going to Heaven, that means you are disqualified. But out of kindness, what did God do? He poured out His love through Jesus Christ and saved us, in spite of ourselves. And I don't know about you, but I'd say that's pretty kind! But herein lies our problem. We live in a world that no longer pleads for the kindness of God. People today no longer think they're disobedient fools, enslaved to sin, and full of hatred. They think they're full of sugar and spice and everything nice, right?

I mean, stop and think about it. The average person today doesn't think they need kindness from God. They think they're owed the Kingdom of God! But, as we've been seeing, if we got what was owed to us, what would we get? We wouldn't pass go and we wouldn't collect $200. We'd go straight to hell! Therefore, let's get a better understanding of Biblical love by taking a closer look at the kindness of God.

The 1st way the Bible reveals the Lovingkindness of God is that God Takes Sinners Just as They Are. Aren't you glad that when you came to Christ it wasn't, okay I got to clean up my act. Now I've got to start being good for a while. Now I've got to stop doing this and that. He just took you as you were. Warts and all, sin and all, pig slop and all. In fact, that may be a stumbling block for some people. They think they have to clean up their act first. No. He will take you the way you are. That's awesome! Guess what? If He didn't do that none of us would have gotten saved.

1 Corinthians 1:26-30: "Brothers, think of what you were when you were called. Not many of you were wise by human standards; not many were influential; not many were of noble birth. But God chose the foolish things of the world to shame the wise. God chose the weak things of the world to shame the strong. He chose the lowly things of this world and the despised things – and the things that are not – to nullify the things that are, so that no one may boast before him. It is because of Him that you are in Christ Jesus."

So here we see when it came to salvation, God chose the WHO? He chose the foolish, the weak, the lowly, and the despised. And guess who that is? That's you and me folks! And why did God do that? Was He just trying to ruin our self-esteem? Absolutely! To keep us from boasting before Him. But not only that, He did it to display His kindness by not waiting for us to become perfect people. Why? Because stop and think about it. If God were to wait for you and me to become perfect, He'd still be waiting, right? I mean who is a perfect person?

But seriously, this is the great news! Out of kindness, God takes you and I, sinners, just as we are, and then He sent Jesus to die in our place. And I don't know about you, but I'd say that's pretty kind, don't you think? And this is why all this self-love, self-esteem teaching going

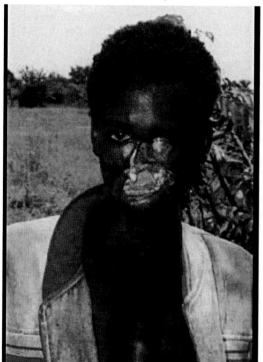

around is so deadly. It actually gets people to boast about their so-called wonderfulness, when the whole time they are filled with wretchedness.

And it seduces people to lose any sense of appreciation for the kindness of God. Now to help illustrate this, this self-help, self-esteem, it helps denigrate the love of God. Because when you see how we must have appeared before a Holy and Righteous God, what does our sin look like? The Bible teaches that the stench of the sins of the people reach His nostrils, how grotesque sin must be to a Holy, Holy God. Do you have any idea how that must be? And you go around, kissing your arm, because of how wonderful you are, God just has to save you, because you are so loving and wonderful. And to help illustrate my point I want you to look at this picture. I came across this picture years ago in a missionary magazine. This is a true story of a kid from Africa. The picture was taken by missionaries. As you can see, he had an accident. His nose, his lips and half of his face was torn off as a child by a hyena attack. If that's not bad enough, here's the backside of that story. That boy has no idea of the awfulness of his condition, because there's no mirrors in the village. Therefore, he's never seen the ugly scars because he's never seen his reflection. And the villagers never say anything. They just love him, like he is nothing different. Isn't that wild?

Now imagine that boy going around that village saying you have to love me, I have to be loved by you people, because I am so handsome and beautiful. I want to be on "GQ." And you're going dude, I love ya, but I don't want to let the cat out of the bag. It's completely out of place.

Here's my point. That's what self-love, self-esteem teaching is. And it's all over the church. The stench of our sins in the nostrils of God, our depravity, the grossness of that, how putrid that must be to God, grotesque it must be, if we were to look at God in His Holiness, and demand that I deserve to be saved. Christ had to die on the cross because we were so worthy. That is false teaching, and this is in the church. No, I don't think so. His loving kindness He takes us just as we are. Compare it to Holy, Holy, Holy, and what that must feel like in God's eyes.

But here's the good news. In spite of our condition, just like those villagers did with that boy, God takes us just as we are, ugliness and all. He looks beyond our deformities, and out of kindness, He still draws us into a relationship with Him. Is that incredible or what? Talk about the love of God! And to think that it's not only free for the asking, but we don't deserve it! Now that's what I call love, how about you?

The 2nd way the Bible reveals the Lovingkindness of God is that God turns sinners into saints.

Romans 1:1,7: "Paul, a servant of Christ Jesus, called to be an apostle and set apart for the gospel of God. To all in Rome who are loved by God and called to be saints. Grace and peace to you from God our Father and from the Lord Jesus Christ."

So here we have the Apostle Paul writing to the Christians in Rome and he not only tells them that they're loved by God, but what? They're called saints of God! Is that incredible or what? I mean, who lives like a saint? Well in case you still don't get it, I'll repeat myself. What we see in the text is out of kindness, God not only takes sinners just as they are, but He takes sinners and turns them into saints! And for those of you who may not know, the word "saint" means "holy ones" or literally "a most holy thing." And I don't know about you, but most of the things we do, they aren't very holy, are they? So, here's the point. How in the world could God call every Christian a saint, a most holy thing? Well, the Bible says God not only accepts us for who we are, and He not only forgives us of our sins, but get this, as we saw earlier, He chooses to forget our sins!

Hebrews 10:16-17: "This is the covenant I will make with them after that time, says the Lord. I will put my laws in their hearts, and I will write them on their minds." Then he adds: "Their sins and lawless acts I will remember no more."

This is what is so incredible about our relationship with God. He not only forgives our sins; He chooses to forget our sins! And because of this, in His eyes, it's as if we never sinned, or in other words, we're a saint! Can you believe that? Is that incredible or what? One guy puts it this way...

"Father love at its best was the love that was revealed from God when Jesus came into the world. And that's why Jesus taught us to pray this way, 'Our Father, Who art in heaven...'

Now you probably know that the word 'father' that Jesus used in the Aramaic language was a very special word. It's the word, 'Abba' which means, 'Daddy.'

God was no longer to be thought of as some sort of transcendental being, demanding his pound of flesh, far removed from us. Instead, God, was supposed to be somebody, who like a Daddy, would gather us up and love us, love us like His very own children.

Now you say, 'I'm not sure God would accept me. You know there's sin in my life.'

Indeed, there is. But that's what the good news of the Gospel is all about. When Jesus came into their world, He came into the world, sent by God, to take away our sin, just so the Father could hug us.

He came to remove the sin, just so that we would be acceptable to the Father. And the Scripture says that if we come to the Father, because of Jesus, He will in no wise cast...us...out! Incredibly good news! And I would agree. Isn't it incredible what God has done for us?"

I mean, stop and think about it.

It's one thing to accept people for who they are. And it's one thing to forgive people for who they are. But to go ahead and treat them as if they'd never sinned, and then hug them like they were your very own children? That's out of this world! But this is the great news. That's exactly what Jesus did when He shed His blood on the cross. And by the way, when it comes to the blood of Jesus, most people think it's kind of strange. In fact, one doctor before he got saved had the same problem. He said this.

"I used to think it strange that the Bible kept talking about the cleansing power of the blood. It seemed to me that blood was messy stuff. In fact, my white lab coats always got stained with blood and it was a chore to get them clean.

But now I understand about the cleansing power of blood. Not because of what blood does on the outside, but on the inside. You see, blood in our bodies has a very important job.

Its constantly cleansing every cell, and constantly washes away all the debris that accumulates inside of us."

And this is what the blood of Jesus does for our sins. And this is why we can be called saints, even though we don't act like it. This is why God can hug us right now, like we were His kids! It's all because the blood of Jesus continually cleanses us from our sins. Therefore, God doesn't see us as we see ourselves. No! He looks at us through those rose-colored glasses and He no longer sees us in our sins, He only sees a saint. Isn't that amazing? And to think that it's not only free for the asking, but we don't deserve it! Now that's what I call love, how about you?

The 3rd way the Bible reveals the Lovingkindness of God is that God turns sinners into sons. He takes you as you are. He turns sinners into saints, and now He says, you are my child. Now let's explore that child analogy a little further. Is it just a convenient idea or is it really a Theological truth?

Ephesians 1:4-6: "Long ago, even before He made the world, God loved us and chose us in Christ to be Holy and without fault in his eyes. His unchanging plan has always been to adopt us into His own family by bringing us to Himself through Jesus Christ. And this gave him great pleasure. So, we praise God for the wonderful kindness He has poured out on us because we belong to His dearly loved Son."

So here we see God not only accepts us for who we are, He not only forgives us of our sin, He not only calls us saints, but He what? He adopts us into His family. He turns sinners into saints! We really do become His children! When He hugs us as children, it's really because we're His children! Isn't that incredible! I mean, who lives like a son of God? Okay, you know the routine. What we see in the text, is that out of kindness, God not only sent Jesus to die for our sins, but He adopts us as His very own children! Can you believe that? Stop and think about it!

There was this couple that I knew while I was in Bible College. They weren't Christians. They were looking into adopting a child because they couldn't have children. There was this one young child who was troubled, disturbed. He told me that this child would take his remains out of the toilet and smear it on the walls. This child had really had a bad life. He was messed up and frankly, needed somebody to love him. To show him some kindness. Show mercy, compassion, and kindness. Show what love really is. But the response was, this person was irate. Why would you even show us that as an option? That's sick. Who would want a child like that?

Go back to our sins. How many messes do we make as Christians. We make a mess all over the place, and we keep on doing it. And aren't you glad God doesn't say, who would want to adopt that child? I want nothing to do with you, are you crazy. We'll take one that is more well behaved. But God takes us. Even with our smeary sins. They probably stink to Him. He takes us as we are. He says that He's not going to give us what we deserve. I'm going to clean you up, inside and out. I'm never going to bring that stuff up ever again. You'll never hear it from My lips, what are you talking about? Oh, and by the way I will adopt you and you will be in My family forever and ever. And then the church says oh, no, that's you crazy fundamental Christians. What the world needs to hear is this real definition of God's love. That you can be a cat or a homosexual or a transvestite or any sinful behavior. We're never going to talk about it. When we actually need to own up to our sin, which is the first step of God's love, His mercy, compassion, and kindness. It's not just wrong, it's not just twisting the truth, it's taken the core out of the gospel, the aspect of God's love and flipped it around into something that is grotesque.

I mean, who in their right mind would take people who sinned against you, didn't want to have anything to do with you, and basically hated your guts, and then turn around and adopt them as one of your very own kids? Now that's what I call love! That's what I call kindness. And it's the same level of kindness this father showed for this person.

This is a letter written to a man on death row by the father of the man whom the man on death row had killed:

"You are probably surprised that I, of all people, am writing a letter to you, but I ask you to read it in its entirety and consider its request seriously. As the father of the man whom you took part in murdering, I have something very important to say to you. I forgive you. With all my heart, I forgive you.

I realize it may be hard for you to believe, but I really do. At your trial, when you confessed to your part in the events that cost My Son His life and asked for My forgiveness, I immediately granted you that forgiveness from My heart.

But this is not all I have to say to you. I want to make you an offer – I want you to become My adopted child. You see, My Son who died was My only child, and I now want to share My life with you.

This may not make sense to you or anyone else, but I have arranged matters so that if you will receive My offer of forgiveness, not only will you be pardoned for your crime, but you'll also be set free from your sentence of death.

And at that point, you will become My adopted child and heir to all my riches. Also, I realize it may seem foolish to make such an offer to one who cost my Son His life, but I now have a great love in My heart for you.

I know you never will be perfect, but you do not have to be perfect to receive My offer. Some would call me foolish for My offer to you, but I wish for you to call Me your Father.

Sincerely,

The Father of Jesus

Now, that's exactly the kind of love God has shown to each one of us. You see, the gospel's not just about God being willing to forgive us of our sins. And it's not just about God being willing to forget our sins. And it's not even about God bringing us into His family. What's amazing about the gospel is that He does it for those who killed His very own Son. And that's why if we can't seem to appreciate that God takes sinners just as they are, He turns them into saints, and adopts them as His very own sons, then something is terribly wrong with us! Why?

Because if we had any idea of the depths of God's love, not a day would go by where we weren't filled with an incredible joy, and we'd shout it from the rooftops to every man, woman, girl or boy! It's right there in the Bible. It's His love letter to us, like this shows:

"My child,

'You may not know Me, but I know everything about you.' **Book of Psalms**

'I know when you sit down and when you rise up. I am familiar with all your ways. For you were made in My image.' **Book of Genesis**

'You are My offspring.' **Book of Acts**

'You were not a mistake. For all your days are written in My book.' **Book of Psalms**

'I determined the exact time of your birth and where you would live.' **Book of Acts**

'My plan for your future has always been filled with hope.' **Book of Jeremiah**

'My thoughts toward you are countless as the sand on the seashore.' **Book of Psalms**

'And I rejoice over you with singing.' **Book of Jeremiah**

'When you are brokenhearted, I am close to you.' **Book of Psalms**

'As a shepherd carries a lamb, I have carried you close to My heart.' **Book of Jeremiah**

'One day I will wipe away every tear from your eyes. And I'll take away all the pain you have suffered on this earth.' **Book of Revelation**

'I gave up everything I loved that I might gain your love.' **Book of Romans**

'My question is: Will you be My child? I am waiting for you.' **Book of Luke**

Love,

Your Dad. Almighty God

When we say those words, when we sing those words, when you read them in the Scripture, I hope it's not just passe for you. I am a child of God. It's all true, it's right there in the Bible, God's love letter to us. Won't you become His child? Or, if you are His child, don't forget it! That's why Jesus came. So that we could become the children of God, and God could hug us as His very own. That's the Lovingkindness of God. Amen?

Chapter Four

God's Love is Gracious & Patient

I don't know about you, but I'd say that God's love is an awesome kind of love! With what we have seen in the previous chapter, you would think that there couldn't be more. But that's not all there is.

The 4th way the Bible reveals that God Is Love is that God gives us graciousness, or that's where we get the word grace. But hey, don't take my word for it. Let's listen to God's. What is this aspect of God's love that He gives us? We all know that we are saved by grace through faith, but let's grab the context. How many times does God say that this is what He does for us?

Ephesians 2:4-10: "But because of His great love for us, God, who is rich in mercy, made us alive with Christ, even when we were dead in transgressions – it is by grace you have been saved. And God raised us up with Christ and seated us with Him in the Heavenly realms in Christ Jesus, in order that in the coming ages He might show the incomparable riches of His grace, expressed in his kindness to us in Christ Jesus. For it is by grace you have been saved, through faith – and this not from yourselves, it is the gift of God – not by works, so that no one can boast. For we are God's workmanship, created in Christ Jesus to do good works, which God prepared in advance for us to do."

Isn't that great! He not only saves you by grace, but He saves you to do something fantastic! Now, according to our text, you can't get any plainer than that. The Bible clearly says that nobody is getting to Heaven because they're so wonderful, or they worked for it, right? Nobody is getting to Heaven because they are good. Nobody is getting to Heaven because they went to church services. What did the text say? We get there purely by the grace of God, right? You can't buy it, you can't earn it, it's simply offered as a free gift. And for those of you who may not know, God's grace is His free gift of giving everything for nothing, to those who don't deserve anything! And actually, what we do deserve is to go to hell because the wages of sin is death.

Now I don't know about you, but I'd say that's being pretty gracious. But that's only half of the story. What you've got to understand is that God not only gives us His grace to get saved, but He gives us grace even after we're saved. You talk about love; this is mind blowing. He gives us grace to love Him, and to serve Him, and obey Him, even after we are saved. He not only keeps us from damnation and hell, but He is gracious. He gives us grace to be saved. And He gives us the ability to live for Him like we should. Why? Because even though we should live for God, especially after all He's done for us, most of the time we don't! And instead of nuking us for our wrong doings, He gives us grace to do what is right! Now that's what I call love! Therefore, in order to better appreciate the love of God, I think we'd better take a closer look at the grace of God. It's pretty simple.

The 1st way the Bible reveals the graciousness of God is that He gives us the ability to obey Him when we can't. Now, think about this. After all He's done for us.

Philippians 2:12-13: "Dearest friends, you were always so careful to follow my instructions when I was with you. And now that I am away, you must be even more careful to put into action God's saving work in your lives, obeying God with deep reverence and fear. For God is working in you, giving you the desire to obey Him, and the power to do what pleases Him."

Now, according to our text, when it comes to obedience to God, who is actually responsible for it? Who is actually doing the work there? It's God, right? What did the text say? God not only gives us the desire to obey, but He gives us the power to obey. I mean, is that incredible or what? Stop and think about what's going on here. You would think that someone who has freely been saved from eternal destruction in hell would naturally want to obey the person responsible for doing that, right? But what do we oftentimes see? Even after being a recipient of the grace of God, we still don't want to obey God, right? Can you imagine the sinfulness of that? Can you imagine if God treated us like we treat Him, after all He's done?

Well, in case you can't, I'm here to help you out. Let's imagine what it would be like if God treated us like we do to Him.

WHAT IF ...

What if - God couldn't take the time to Bless us today because we couldn't take the time to thank Him yesterday?

What if - God decided to stop leading us tomorrow because we didn't follow Him today?

What if – God didn't walk with us today because we failed to recognize it was His day?

What if - God stopped loving and caring for us because we failed to love and care for others?

What if – God took away the Bible tomorrow, because we wouldn't read it today?

What if – the door to the Church Sanctuary was closed because we didn't open the door of our hearts?

What if – God wouldn't hear us today because we wouldn't listen to Him yesterday?

What if – God answered our prayers the way we answer His call to service?

What if – God met our needs the way we give Him our lives?

Now, I don't know about you, but I'm so glad God doesn't treat us like we treat Him, Amen?

The facts are, we're not only saved by the grace of God, but we walk, live, and breathe the grace of God every single day! We are immersed in it 24 hours a day, 7 days a week! And the point is this. If we had any idea the depths of which God is being gracious to us, it would empower us to obey Him, no matter the circumstance, even when it seems impossible, like it did with this man.

"David McAllister is a blind, 77-year-old ex-convict, who 22 years ago kidnapped 10-year-old Chris Carrier, shot him, and left him for dead, in the Florida Everglades.

Although blinded in his left eye by the bullet, the boy survived. However, David McAllister escaped, and for more than two decades the case went unsolved.

That is until last fall when a distraught McAllister, his frail body bedridden in a Miami nursing home, confessed to the crime. And after learning of the confession, Carrier, now 32, visited McAllister at his nursing home.

But Chris did not go in anger or bitterness. Rather, in obedience to God, he went to pray with his would-be murderer and share the good news of how Jesus had transformed his own life."

Now, I don't know about you, but man, if most of us were ol' Chris there, the last thing we'd want to do is to share the love of God with the person who tried to kill us, you know what I mean? This really happened, this is our brother in Christ. But here's the good news. God isn't like you and me. He doesn't treat us like we treat Him, or even how we treat each other. Out of graciousness, He not only came to save us from our sins, but He came to give us the ability to live a life that pleases Him. Whether you realize it or not, God wants us to obey Him by sharing His love with others, even if it means our own would-be killer. Why? Because that's the same kind of love He's given to us. And the point is this. We all know we should be willing to do this naturally, but God knows we can't! So, what does He do? Does he nuke us? No! He gives us the grace so we can! Is that incredible or what? Talk about the love of God!

Oh, but that's not all. The 2nd way the Bible reveals the graciousness of God, is that He gives us the ability to serve Him when we won't. After all He's done, and we make up excuses why we can't serve Him.

1 Corinthians 12:1,4-6,11 "And now, dear brothers and sisters, I will write about the special abilities the Holy Spirit gives to each of us, for I must correct your misunderstandings about them. Now there are different kinds of spiritual gifts, but it is the same Holy Spirit who is the source of them all. There are different kinds of service in the Church, but it is the same Lord we are serving. There are different ways God works in our lives, but it is the same God who does the work through all of us. He alone decides which gift each person should have."

Wait a minute, you mean I just wasted my time buying that book at the prayer and fasting conference, with meals provided, to try to learn the secret thing? If I jump up and down, and do all these techniques, I can get the gift that I want? You just wasted your time and money. Now, according to our text, when it comes to serving God, who is actually responsible for it? It's God, right? What did the text say? God not only gives us gifts to serve Him, but He alone decides which gifts we get to serve Him with. I mean, is that incredible or what? Stop and think about what's going on here.

You would think that someone who has freely been saved from eternal destruction in hell would naturally want to serve the person responsible, for doing that, right? But folks, what do we often see, even as Christians? Even after being a recipient of the grace of God, we not only don't want to be obedient to God, but half the time, we don't even want to serve God. Can you imagine the sinfulness of that? And as if that wasn't bad enough, even if we are finally getting around to "so-called" serving God, we still blow it by treating it like a boring job instead of a loving ministry. And in case you don't know the difference between the two, I came across a test. Let's see if our service to God is a job, or a ministry.

IS IT A JOB OR A MINISTRY?

If you do it because no one else will, it's a job. If you are doing it to serve the Lord, it's a ministry.

If you do it just enough to get by, it's a job. If you do it to the best of your ability, it's a ministry.

If you quit because someone criticized you, it was a job. If you keep serving, it's a ministry.

If you quit because no one praised you, it was a job. If you do it because you think it needs to be done, it's a ministry.

If your concern is just success, it's a job. If your concern is faithfulness to God, it's a ministry.

It's hard to get excited about a job. It's almost impossible not to get excited about a ministry.

Average churches are filled with many people doing many jobs. Great churches are filled with many people who are involved in ministry.

People may say, "Well done," when you do your job. But the Lord will say, "Well, done, thou good and faithful servant." when you complete your ministry.

I'm so glad that God doesn't treat us like we treat Him! I mean think of the audacity here. The same people who've been saved from hell, by the grace of God, look upon serving Him out of guilt or as a boring job! Oh, but we don't stop there! We'll even start making excuses! We say stuff like, "Well, I just don't know if I have the time...I'll see if I can fit it in my calendar." Or "I don't know if I'm good enough, I'm not qualified. How about getting somebody else who has better skills?" And on and on it goes! We are all different. Scripture says that we are all given different gifts. Every one of us is important. Every gift is important. All of it adds to the collective whole of Christ. But the point is, use what God's given to you as a talent for His glory and the edification of others, like this girl from Romania.

A young girl is sitting behind a piano at a place that looks like a program like "America's Got Talent." When the camera rewinds a minute, you can see her walking to the piano. She has on a pretty dress and her hair is done nicely on top of her head. But when you look closer you will see that she has no arms. She sits in a tall chair so that her toes can easily touch the keyboard. She starts touching the keys and a beautiful song is played. Her family in the wings are trying to hold back emotion while she plays. Her name is Lorelai Mosnegotu and she is 14 years old. Then she starts to sing the words to the song that she is playing. She has a beautiful voice, and the audience starts to applaud. The judges are shaking their heads and wiping away tears. This is unbelievable. She finishes her song. She bows to the audience and the judges, and then walks off the stage.

Now if anybody had an excuse not to serve God, and other people, it's got to be that girl, right? But what'd she do? She figured out a way to use her God-given abilities to sing anyway, and even learned to play piano with her toes! She was not going to let anything stop her! And so should it be with us! Especially after all God's done for us, namely, saving us from hell! Isn't that good enough? What more does He have to do to motivate us to serve Him? If we had any idea the depths of which God is being gracious to us, it would empower us to serve Him no matter the circumstance, even when it seems impossible, like it did with this man.

"Charlie Hainline is a layman at Coral Ridge Presbyterian Church in Fort Lauderdale, Florida. He is a man who radiates the love of Christ and is serious about sharing his faith with others.

One year, his goal was to serve God by leading 1650 people to faith in Christ (5 a day)!! Once, he was out witnessing with a couple of other folks, and though he didn't share the gospel, he sat there and smiled as a teammate did.

But, when the teammate was finished and asked if the person would like to trust Christ, and receive the gift of eternal life, the person replied, "If being a Christian would make me like him (pointing to Charlie), I want it!"

But what you need to understand is that Charlie's life wasn't always full of joy, nor a bed of roses by any means. His daughter was kidnapped, killed, and her head was found floating in a canal.

And when the murderer of his daughter was caught and convicted, Charlie went to jail in order to share the love of God to that man."

Now, I don't know about you, but if most of us were ol' Charlie there, the last thing we'd want to do is to share the love of God with the person who killed our daughter and chopped her head off, you know what I mean? But people, here's the good news. God isn't like you and I. Out of graciousness, He not only came to save us from our sins, but He came to give us the ability to live a life that pleases Him, like Charlie. Whether you realize it or not, God wants us to serve Him by sharing His love with others, even if it means our own daughter's killer. Why? Because that's the same kind of love He's given to us. We all know we should be willing to do this naturally, but God knows we can't! So, what does He do? Does he nuke us? No! He gives us the grace so we can! Is that incredible or what? Talk about the love of God! And to think that it's not only free for the asking, but we don't deserve it! Now that's what I call love, how about you?

Oh, but that's not all. The 3rd way the Bible reveals the graciousness of God is that He gives us the ability to love Him when we don't.

1 John 4:16,17,19 "And so we know and rely on the love God has for us. God is love. Whoever lives in love lives in God, and God in him. In this way, love is made complete among us so that we will have confidence on the day of judgment, because in this world we are like Him. We love because He first loved us."

According to our text, when it comes to loving God, who is actually responsible for it? It's God, right? What did the text say? God not only gives us His love, but it's because of His love we have the ability to love Him in return. I mean, is that incredible or what? Stop and think about what's going on here. You would think that someone who has freely been saved from eternal destruction in hell would naturally want to love the person responsible for doing that, right? But folks, what do we often see, even as Christians? Even after being a recipient of the grace of God, we not only don't want to be obedient to God, we not only don't want to serve God, but half the time we don't even want to love God. Can you imagine how horrible that is? And to show you how horrible this kind of behavior is, let's take a look at another kind of love. Let's take a look at the love of a dog.

Now, first of all, dogs are cool! If you like cats, we'll pray for you. I hear some people love them. And I hear they taste like chicken! But dogs, they'll do just about anything, just to be around their Master. Not cats, they're snooty! They say, "Look at me, I'm the master." Not dogs, they jump on you, in fact, sometimes, dogs will even dance with you! Like this dog. You can't get a cat to do this.

In the background they are playing bongo drums. A young guy is swinging and swaying in time with the music. Standing in front of him, a little white dog is also swinging and swaying his rear end. He is so into the music that his whole body is beginning to move, his tail is wagging, and he opens his mouth as if to start singing also.

Now how many of you want that dog? I do! You're not going to get a cat to do that! But this is what dogs do! They love you; they'll jump on you, they lick you, they kiss you, they just want to be around you! Every time you come home, what does the dog do? He goes nuts! He can't believe it. It's absolutely amazing to him that you're even home again. And just walking in the door almost kills him. It's as if the dog is saying, "He's back again! It's that guy! It's that guy! Yippee!" You leave the house for 30 seconds and come back in, and he does it all over again! Dogs are loyal, they care for you. In fact, they have this innate sense to rescue someone, or something in harm's way, like this dog did.

A BEST FRIEND. A HERO.

Narrator: *"This is truly amazing. Here's a dog that has been hit by a car trying to cross the road. He's hit and just lying in the middle of this busy highway, and a second dog spots him and tries to get over to him. Here again is the first dog being hit. He's lying there in the middle of the road, a busy time of day, and here comes the second dog, who grabs him, not by his teeth, but gets him by his paws, by his neck, and drags him in the middle of all this traffic, off the road to safety. Little by little, inch by inch. Finally, some workers spot the dog, and come over and help them. And by the way, the injured dog lived."*

Wow! Almost makes you want to weep. This is what dogs do inherently! Turn to somebody and say, "You ain't going to get no cat to do that!" Dogs are awesome! They love, they serve, they save, and they even obey their master's implicitly, like this dog did. One guy said this, and this is a true story also.

"Archibald Rutledge wrote that one day he met a man whose dog had just been killed in a forest fire. And obviously heartbroken, the man explained to Rutledge how it happened.

Because he worked outdoors, he often took his dog with him. And on that particular morning, he left the animal in a clearing, and gave him a command to stay, and watch his lunch bucket while he went into the forest.

His faithful friend understood, for that's exactly what he did. Then a fire started in the woods, and soon the blaze spread to the spot where the dog had been left. But he didn't move. He stayed right where he was, in perfect obedience to his master's word.

And with tearful eyes, the dog's owner said, "I always had to be careful what I told him to do, because I knew he would do it out of love."

Here we have a dog, lovingly being obedient to his master, even unto death, yet many Christians refuse to love their Heavenly Master who saved them from death. They don't serve, they don't obey, they don't even love God like a dog does for his master. And can I tell you something? That dog is a better Christian than you! You don't obey Jesus, you don't serve Jesus, you don't love Jesus, you won't dance with Him, you don't long to be with Him, and He says, "Come! Follow Me!" and you say, "NO!" Something's wrong with that picture! The facts are that most of the time we can't even show the same level of love to God, as a dog does to a man, even after all He's done for us! And I don't know about you, but most of us would nuke the person on the spot! Not God! What does He do? Out of graciousness He empowers us to love Him, not because we have to, but because we want to, like it was with this lady.

"There was a man who was a tyrant, and he insisted that his wife get up real early every single morning to prepare his breakfast. He was very demanding with regard to her care of the house, he required a strict

accounting of the money spent on groceries, clothes for the children, etc. Then one day he died.

Well, later she married a man who was just the opposite. He was loving, tender, considerate, unselfish. And one day she was going through some of the papers of her first husband and found a list of all the things he had required her to do.

Then to her amazement, she realized she was doing all those things for her present husband, but without being required to do them. She realized that she was doing them voluntarily because she loved him."

Now, the reason why I like that illustration, is because I think it's how many Christians look at their relationship with God. They think of Him as that first man there. They think He's just a big ol' tyrant who just wants slavish obedience, or they're going to get it. But that's not God! He's not like you and me. He's gracious! Even though He should treat us like that tyrant, and nuke us on the spot for not loving Him, what's He do? He knows we can't love Him like He deserves, so He gives us grace to love Him in return! Is that incredible or what? Talk about the love of God! And that's why if we can't seem to appreciate that God not only saves us, by His grace, but He also gives us the ability to love, serve, and obey Him, by His grace, then something is terribly wrong with us! Why? Because if we had any idea of the depths of God's love, we'd have a smile on our face that nothing could tame, and we couldn't stop our lips from praising His Name! Why? Because that's what happens when you truly begin understanding the graciousness of God. Amen?

The 5th way the Bible reveals that God Is Love is that God Gives Us Patience. But hey, don't take my word for it. Let's listen to God's.

II Peter 3:5-9: "But they deliberately forget that long ago by God's word the Heavens existed and the earth was formed out of water and by water. By these waters also the world of that time was deluged and destroyed. By the same word, the present heavens and earth are reserved for fire, being kept for the day of judgment and destruction of ungodly men. But do not forget this one thing, dear friends, with the Lord a day is like a thousand years, and a thousand years are like a day. The Lord is not slow in keeping his promise, as some understand slowness. He is patient with you, not wanting anyone to perish, but everyone to come to repentance."

Now, according to our text, we've got some good news and we've got some not so good news. And the not so good news is that God's not done punishing mankind for his wickedness, right? What did the text say? The first time it was a worldwide flood, but the second time it's going to be what? A worldwide fire, right? But praise God, there's some good news as well. What did the text say? In spite of man's continual wickedness, God is patient with people, putting up with their wickedness day, after day, after day! Why? Because He doesn't want them to perish! He wants them to repent, and get saved, right? And I don't know about you, but I'd say that's being pretty patient. But once again, that's only half of the story.

What you've got to understand is that God's not only patient with our sins until we get saved, but He's also patient with our sins even after we're saved. Now that's what I call love! Therefore, in order to better appreciate the love of God, I think we'd better take a closer look at the patience of God. And it's pretty simple.

The 1st way the Bible reveals the patience of God is that He puts up with our continual slavery.

Romans 6:1-2,6-7 "Well then, should we keep on sinning so that God can show us more and more kindness and forgiveness? Of course not! Since we have died to sin, how can we continue to live in it? Our old sinful selves were crucified with Christ so that sin might lose its power in our lives. We are no longer slaves to sin. For when we died with Christ, we were set free from the power of sin."

According to our text, it's pretty clear. When it comes to the issue of sin, Jesus not only came to forgive us of it, but to set us free from it. Do you have any idea what this means? It means that for the first time, we have the ability, through the Holy Spirit, to just say no to sin. And now, we don't have to sin like we used to. Why? Because we're no longer slaves to sin! We actually have a choice! Is that incredible or what? But we've got a problem. You see, even though God's given us the ability to sin less, what do we do? We sin even more! Can you believe that? And the point is this. You would think that someone who has freely been saved from eternal destruction in hell would naturally want to stop sinning against the person responsible for doing that, right? But what do we see? Even after all God's done, we don't just say no to sin. No! What do we do? We say yes to sin again, and again. We listen to satan say "OK" when God says no…wrong answer! Like this little kid!

A little boy is standing in front of the class looking at the chalkboard. He has an equation written on the board, and he has to write down the correct answer. The equation is 2 + 1 =, he is stumped. He turns around to look at the kids at their desks and one little girl holds up three fingers. He didn't count the three fingers, he looked at the way she held up her fingers. The symbol was also a sign for OK. So, he wrote down the answer to the equation 2 + 1 = OK. And then he runs back to his desk.

No dude, no! It's THREE! Wrong answer! Anybody know somebody like that? But folks, that's no different than us when we say "OK" to satan and sinning, and God says, "No, no, no! Wrong answer!" and He shakes His head! Can you imagine how horrible that is? Sinning against God again? Listening to satan? Well, just in case you can't, let's take a look at what the Bible has to say about this kind of behavior.

2 Peter 2:21-22 "It would be better if they had never known the right way to live than to know it and then reject the holy commandments that were given to them. They make these proverbs come true: 'A dog returns to its vomit.'"

Whether you realize it or not, when we keep on sinning again, and again, even after we've been saved, we are in essence choosing vomit over God. We're choosing a pile of puke over Christ! Can you believe it? Oh, but that's not all folks! It gets worse! In the book of Romans, the Apostle Paul used a peculiar phrase to describe his joy about being set free from the slavery of sin. He said, "Praise be to God who rescued me from this body of death!" Now, in order to appreciate Paul's comment here, we need to take a look at what a "body of death" was back in those days.

"It is reported that there was an actual Roman custom that sentenced convicted murderers to an especially gruesome execution. Their unique sense of justice included strapping the dead body of the person they murdered to the back of the murderer.

Then the criminal would then be forced to drag the decomposing corpse with him wherever he went. And in just a few days, which doubtless seemed an eternity to the convicted man, the decay of the person he had killed would start to infect his own body, until he was killed in return.

And it is believed that this was the torture that Paul had in mind when he expressed his joy of being freed from "the body of death."

I don't know about you, but I wouldn't want to walk around with a dead stinking body on my back, you know what I mean? But whether you realize it or not, when we keep on sinning again and again, even after we've been saved, we are in essence choosing a dead body over God! We're choosing a stinking corpse over Christ! Can you believe that? Let's put it in context. How would you feel if somebody kept choosing a pile of vomit over you? How would you feel if somebody kept choosing a dead stinking rotten corpse over you? Let's be honest. If somebody treated us like that, what would we do? We'd nuke 'em on the spot, right? How much more God? But here's the good news. God isn't like you and me! He's patient!

And out of patience, He not only forgives us of our sin, but He puts up with our sin again, and again, and again! Every single day! And to think the whole time, He doesn't have to! Especially after all He's done! Now that's what I call love!

Oh, but that's not all. The 2nd way the Bible reveals the patience of God is that He puts up with our continual idolatry.

1 John 2:15-16 "Stop loving this evil world and all that it offers you, for when you love the world, you show that you do not have the love of the Father in you. For the world offers only the lust for physical pleasure, the lust for everything we see, and pride in our possessions. These are not from the Father. They are from this evil world."

According to our text, it's pretty clear. When it comes to the issue of idolatry, Jesus not only came to forgive us of it, but He came to tell us to stay away from it, right? What did the text say? Stop loving the things of this world! Why? Because God doesn't want you to spend your time loving things. Are you kidding? He wants you to spend your time loving Him, right? And the point is this. You would think that someone who has freely been saved from eternal destruction in hell would naturally want to stop committing idolatry against the person responsible for doing that, right? But what do we see? Even though we know God wants us to stop loving things, what do we do? We keep on loving things even more! It sounds so good! That's the LIE! You think it's going to taste wonderful! It's all you need …then the truth pops out. Like this guy found out during breakfast.

"I just wanted to eat a banana when I saw something." There was a little spot on the banana that moved. As he kept watching that spot a little hole began to tear where the movement was. The little hole started to get bigger, when suddenly a leg poked through. It was pulled back into the banana, but the hole got bigger, and a spider popped out. "I ate an apple."

Okay, how many of you are never going to eat a banana the rest of your life? Oh yuck! But it looked so good on the outside. Can you believe that? But folks, how is this any different than when we choose idolatry over God? It's looks nice on the outside…it's all we need…more and more…but sooner or later…the truth pops out! It's SIN! In fact, it's a gross sin that will harm you! One author put it this way.

"Leo Tolstoy once wrote a story about a successful peasant farmer who wasn't satisfied with his lot in life. He wanted more of everything. And one day he received an offer.

For 1000 rubles, he could buy all the land he could walk around in a day. The only catch in the deal was that he had to be back at his starting point by sundown. So early the next morning he started out walking at a fast pace.

And even though by midday he was getting very tired, he kept on going, covering more and more ground. But well into the afternoon he realized that his greed had taken him very far from the starting point. So, he quickened his pace as the sun began to sink low in the sky.

He realized he had to make it back before sundown or he'd lose all the land he just gained, so he began to run faster and faster. And just as the sun began to sink below the horizon, he came within sight of the finish line.

And gasping for breath, his heart pounding, he called upon every bit of strength left in his body and staggered across the line just before the sun disappeared. However, the man immediately collapsed, blood streaming from his mouth. In a few minutes he was dead.

And afterwards, his servants dug a grave. Oh, the man got his land alright. It was about six feet long and three feet wide. The title of the story was: How Much Land Does a Man Need?"

How many things in life do we need? How sad it is that we all joke about the rat race of life and how it only leads to an early grave, yet what do we do? Just like that man, we keep on running it faster, and faster, and faster. And it'll not only kill your physical life but your spiritual life. Why? Because whether you realize it or not, when we keep on loving things again and again, even after we've been saved, we are in essence choosing an early grave over God! We're choosing a casket over Christ! Can you believe it? But that's not all folks! It gets worse. Let's see, not just look, at what an author has to say about this behavior. Let's take a look at what the Bible says about it.

Philippians 3:7-8 "But whatever was to my profit I now consider loss for the sake of Christ. What is more, I consider everything a loss compared to the surpassing greatness of knowing Christ Jesus my Lord, for whose sake I have lost all things. I consider them rubbish, that I may gain Christ."

Now that word "rubbish" is actually the Greek word, "skubalon" and you know what it means? Dog dung.... it's "the excrement of animals." So, here's what Paul is saying. Whether you realize it or not, when we keep on loving things again and again, even after we've been saved, what are we doing? We are in essence choosing a pile of dog dung over God! We're choosing a pile of excrement over Christ! Can you believe that? And once again, let's put it in context.

How would you feel if somebody did that to you? Let's be honest. If somebody treated us like that, what would we do? We'd nuke 'em on the spot, right? How much more God? But people, here's the good news. God isn't like you and me! He's patient! And out of patience, He not only forgives us of our sin, but He puts up with our sin again, and again, and again! Every single day! And to think the whole time, He doesn't have to! Especially after all He's done! Now that's what I call love, how about you?

The 3rd way the Bible reveals the patience of God is that He puts up with our continual harlotry.

Deuteronomy 31:16-17 "And the LORD said to Moses: You are going to rest with your fathers, and these people will soon prostitute themselves to the foreign gods of the land they are entering. They will forsake Me and break the covenant I made with them. On that day I will become angry with them and forsake them; I will hide my face from them, and they will be destroyed."

When it comes to the issue of harlotry, or in other words, selling yourselves out to the world, it's obviously something God doesn't like, right? What did the text say? Prostituting yourself before the world, makes Him what? It makes Him angry, right? Why? Because stop and think about it. It's basically slapping God in the face after all He's done for us. And the point is this. You would think that someone who has freely been saved from eternal destruction in hell would naturally want to stop committing harlotry against the person responsible for doing that, right? But what do we see? Not just the Israelites, but even we Christians sell out to the world system, right? Let's be honest! What does the majority of the American Church do? We spend all our time, treasure, talents, and tongues lusting after the glamour and glitz of this world, right? Of course! Why it's the American dream! From God's perspective, do you have any idea how horrible this behavior must be? Well, in case you can't, let's take a look at what happened to one person who prostituted themselves before this world system.

"All he ever really wanted in life was more. He wanted more money, so he turned some inherited wealth into a billion-dollar pile of assets. He wanted more fame, so he broke into the Hollywood scene and soon became a filmmaker and a star.

He wanted more sensual pleasures, so he paid handsome sums to indulge his every sexual urge. He wanted more thrills, so he designed, built, and piloted the fastest aircraft in the world.

He wanted more power, so he dealt political favors so skillfully that two U.S. presidents became his pawns. All he ever wanted was more. He was absolutely convinced that more of this world system would bring him true satisfaction. Unfortunately, history shows otherwise.

This same man ended his life emaciated and colorless. His chest was sunken in, and his fingernails were grotesque inches-long corkscrews. His body was rotting full of tumors, his teeth were black, and his arms were full of needle marks from his drug addiction.

He died a billionaire junkie, insane by all reasonable standards. His name of course, was Howard Hughes. A man who died believing the myth of more."

I don't know about you, but I don't want to end up like Howard Hughes, do you know what I mean? But I've got a question to ask. If we don't want to end up like Howard Hughes, then why are so many Christians still living for this world system? Why are so many giving all their time, treasure, talents and tongue to everything else in this world, but God? Do we really think He doesn't see this? The facts are, whether you realize it or not, when we sell out to this world system again and again, even after we've been saved, we are in essence choosing an emaciated colorless life over God. We're choosing insanity over Christianity! Can you believe that? It's about as insane as this decision was!

"I enjoy scaring my wife. I'm going to hide in this pile of leaves. Wish me luck."

And he buries himself under the pile of leaves. Everything is going according to plan until his phone starts ringing.

"Really?"

A phone call forced him from his hiding place, just as his wife came home and did this. She ran the car over the pile of leaves.

"Are you kidding me?!"

What's important is that this man learned his lesson.

"And that's why you never pull jokes on your wife. I cannot believe that."

Now, how many of you would say that guy was lucky to escape with his life! Oh, it sounded funny! It sounded cool! But he learned the hard way, don't ever prank your wife! She's going to kill you! How is this any different when we continue to commit slavery, idolatry, and even harlotry against God as Christians? Do we really think we're not going to get run over by a spiritual truck? It will kill us spiritually! How many times does God have to tell us, don't prank around with sin! Again, let's put it in context. How would you feel if somebody did that to you? "Sorry honey, I can't spend time with you. I'd rather get run over by a truck!"

Let's be honest! If somebody treated us like that, what would we do? We'd nuke 'em on the spot, right? How much more God? But here's the good news. God isn't like you and me! He's patient! And out of patience, He not only forgives us of our sin, but He puts up with our sin again, and again, and again! Every single day! And to think the whole time, He doesn't have to! Especially after all He's done! Now that's what I call love, how about you? That's why, if we can't seem to appreciate, that out of patience, God not only saves us from our sins, but He continually puts up with our sins, even after being saved, then something is terribly wrong with us! Why? Because, if we had any idea of the depths of God's love, we'd shut our mouths, and never complain, and tell everyone we meet, you better do the same! Why? Because that's what happens when you truly begin understanding the loving patience of Almighty God! Amen?

Chapter Five

God's Love is
Faithful & Good

Earlier we saw the perversion and the twisting of God's Biblical truth. They say God's love is eros instead of agapao. And that's why they say we should allow any and all sinful behavior. You can't judge anybody, any kind of sexual behavior, any kind of lifestyle, homosexuality, transgender, gender fluidity, it's all acceptable. That is the new definition, in the church. That is what they are saying a loving Christian is. And that is why we began to take a look at what is Biblical love. Remember, God's love is like a diamond, it has different facets. We've seen God reveals He is love by giving us mercy. And that out of mercy, God will give His enemies a palace in Heaven instead of a pit in hell, a body of perfection instead of a body of pain, and a heavenly greeting instead of a hellish goodbye. We also saw that He gives us compassion.

And we saw that out of compassion God not only died for those who wanted Him dead, but He continually forgives our continual sins. Now, is that an awesome kind of love or what? And then He gives us kindness, where He accepts sinners just as they are. He turns them into saints and then He turns them into sons. And then we saw two more. God reveals He is love by giving us graciousness, and out of graciousness God gives us the grace not only to get saved, but He gives us grace to obey, serve, and love Him, even after we're saved!

And then we saw He gives us patience, where out of patience God not only puts up with our sins until we get saved, but He puts up with our sins even after we're saved! Including the sins of loving a pile of puke, a rotting corpse, and a casket over Christ. That is slavery, idolatry, and harlotry. And I'd say that's an awesome kind of love!

But that's not all. The 6th way the Bible reveals that God is love, is that God gives us faithfulness. But hey, don't take my word for it. Let's listen to God's.

1 John 1:5-10: "This is the message we have heard from Him and declare to you. God is light; in Him there is no darkness at all. If we claim to have fellowship with Him, yet walk in the darkness, we lie and do not live by the truth. But if we walk in the light, as He is in the light, we have fellowship with one another and the blood of Jesus, His Son, purifies us from all sin. If we claim to be without sin, we deceive ourselves and the truth is not in us. If we confess our sins, He is faithful and just and will forgive us our sins and purify us from all unrighteousness. If we claim we have not sinned, we make Him out to be a liar and his word has no place in our lives."

Now, once again, according to our text, we've got some good news and we've got some bad news. And the bad news is, if you say you're a Christian and keep walking in sin like it's no big deal, what did the text say? It says you're a liar and you might very well be a phony believer, right? But not only that, it also said if you go to the other extreme and say that you have no sin, then what? You're not only a liar, but you're calling God a liar! And I don't know about you, but I'd say that's probably not a good thing to do. But praise God there's some good news as well. What did the text say? If we would just confess our sins, God is what? He's faithful! And faithful to do what? Beat us over the head with a two-by-four or smack us around? No! He's faithful to forgive us of all our sins, right? Is that incredible or what?

But, once again, that's only half of the story. What you've got to understand is that God not only provides for our spiritual needs, in forgiving us of our sins, get this. He also provides for our practical needs in spite of our sins. Have you ever stopped to think about that? Now I'd say that's being pretty loving, pretty faithful, how about you?

The 1st way the Bible reveals the faithfulness of God is that He keeps handing out His provision.

Matthew 6:25,26,28,30: "So I tell you, don't worry about everyday life – whether you have enough food, drink, and clothes. Look at the birds. They don't need to plant or harvest or put food in barns because your heavenly Father feeds them. And why worry about your clothes? Look at the lilies and how they grow. They don't work or make their clothing. And if God cares so wonderfully for flowers that are here today and gone tomorrow, won't He more surely care for you? You have so little faith!"

So here we see when it comes to the issue of daily provision, Jesus not only promised to provide it for us, but He also said don't you dare worry about it, right? Isn't that incredible? What did the text say? If we just have faith in God's faithfulness, then we can just say goodbye to worry once and for all. What a promise, huh? I mean, that's incredible. But folks, we've got a problem. You see, you'd think that since we naturally trust in God for our eternal salvation, that trusting Him for our daily provision would be a piece of cake, right? But what do we see? Even though God told us not to worry about our provisions, what do we do? We keep on worrying even more! Can you believe that? And if that wasn't bad enough, then we have the audacity to start whining! We whine because we don't have a new car. We whine because we don't have a new house. We whine because we don't have a new job.

And on and on it goes! And it's not just a slap in the face to God, it's absolutely ludicrous! Why? Because God has provided for us! So much so, we are filthy rich in comparison to the rest of the world. And for those of you who may not believe me, let's take a test. Let's see just how rich we really are.

HOW RICH ARE WE?

Take out all the furniture in your house except for one table and a couple chairs. Use a blanket and pads for beds.

Take away all of your clothing except for your oldest dress or suit, shirt or blouse. Leave only one pair of shoes.

Take away the house itself and move the family into the tool shed.

Place your "house" in a shantytown.

Cancel all subscriptions to newspapers, magazines, and book clubs. This is no great loss because none of you can read anyway.

Empty the pantry and the refrigerator except for a small bag of flour, some sugar and salt, a few potatoes, some onions, and a dish of dried beans.

Dismantle the bathroom, shut off the running water, and remove all the electrical wiring in your house.

Leave only one radio for the whole shantytown.

Move the nearest hospital or clinic ten miles away and put a midwife in charge instead of a doctor.

Throw away your bankbooks, stock certificates, pension plans, and insurance policies. Leave the family a cash hoard of ten dollars.

Give the head of the family a few acres to cultivate on which he can raise a few hundred dollars of cash crops, of which one third will go to the landlord and one-tenth to the money lenders.
Lop off twenty-five or more years in life expectancy.

And if you can do all this you will see how daily life is for 1 billion people in the world.

Now, I don't know about you, but I'd say God's doing a pretty good job of providing for us, do you know what I'm saying? I mean, the fact that we have ever even considered going on a diet should tell us something, right? The facts are, we've all got a place to sleep, clothes on our back, and food in our bellies. And yeah, it might get lean sometimes, but I don't see anybody naked or starving around here, do you? Therefore, where do we get off worrying, whining, and complaining about our lives to God? Who do we think we are? It's like a horrible disease that's spreading to even the younger generations, like this girl.

TEENAGE AFFLUENZA

Narrator: *"Deep in the center of the American suburbs lives a 15-year-old girl named Jennie. By all appearances she looks like an average healthy high school student. But at the heart of her tragic story, we find circumstances that are widespread across her peer group around the country. Jennie awakens in her room, every morning, alone, on only a twin size bed. The request to her parents for a larger newer bed continues to fall on deaf ears. Even her cry for bed linens with a higher thread count go unanswered.*

RURAL SOUTHERN AFRICA

Annie lives with her grandmother with her two little sisters in a one room mud hut that has been badly damaged by storms. She sleeps on a grass mat on the hard dirt floor. There is only one blanket for everyone to share.

Sadly, teenagers like Jennie only have an average of $267.00 to spend per month. That's a little more than $65.00 for an entire week. At breakfast, Jennie usually has to fight with her siblings to get the last pop tart in the pantry. On the day she loses the battle she is forced to eat cereal and fresh fruit. The drive to school every day creates yet another clash with siblings for the coveted location in the car known as shotgun in the front passenger seat. Even when Jennie is victorious, she finds herself cold in the leather seats of her family's BMW that lacks seat warmers. To make matters worse, Jennie's mother makes frequent attempts to carry on an actual *conversation with her daughter. Unleashing a barrage of small talk upon Jennie from the driver's seat.*

Annie and her sisters work in the fields to help her grandmother grow corn for their meals. However, their country is suffering from a four-year drought and this year's crop will not yield enough food to carry them through for another year.

In Jennie's closet you will find a serious lack of brand names sewn in dozens of her shirts, jeans and dresses. Shocking, she is made to choose only one purse from Fendi, Gucci, or Louis Vuitton at the mall with her mother.

Annie and her sisters have two dresses each and none of them fit them well. They have holes and are thread barren in some places. After a long day of working in the field, the girls spend their time helping their grandmother repair their dilapidated hut or digging holes in the dry riverbed to get water.

Jennie has found herself in yet another no-win situation. She does her best to remain brave, while choosing between tap water and wholesale bottled water to wet her parched mouth.

When Annie and her sisters do find water in the dry riverbed, it's usually dirty from cows and other animals drinking from the same water hole. There are also other countless bacteria and other microorganisms in the water that can make them very sick.

Don't become a victim of Teenage Affluenza. You only have one life. Do something."

Yes please, we've got to do something. Let's start off by repeating after me. What a stinking brat, right? What an ungrateful teenager! She has no idea how good she's got it, right? But, let's be honest, how is this any different when we do this as adults? "How come I don't have a new car? How come I don't have a new house? How come I don't have a new job, and on and on it goes! We've got Affluenza too! And from God's perspective, do you have any idea how horrible this is? I mean, let's put it into context. How would you feel if you busted your back to take care of your family and nothing you ever did was good enough? How would you like it if you worked your fingers to the bone, and all people ever did was whine and complain about everything?

Let's be honest! If somebody treated us like that, what would we do? We'd tell them to get away from me you ungrateful wretch! Get out of here and provide for yourself if you don't like it, right? Then people, how much more should God say that to you and me? But here's the good news. God isn't like you and me! He's faithful! And out of faithfulness He not only forgives our sins, but He keeps on handing out His provision in spite of our sins! Can you believe that? Now that's what I call love, how about you?

Oh, but that's not all. The 2nd way the Bible reveals the faithfulness of God is that He keeps handing out His protection.

1 Corinthians 10:13: "But remember that the temptations that come into your life are no different from what others experience. And God is faithful. He will keep the temptation from becoming so strong that you can't stand up against it. When you are tempted, He will show you a way out, so that you will not give in to it."

So, here we see when it comes to the issue of daily protection from temptation, God's promised to provide a way out for us, every single time, right? And you'd think someone who's freely been saved from eternal destruction in hell would naturally take God up on His offer to not give into temptation, right? But what do we see? Even though we know God's provided a way out of every single temptation, what do we do? We keep giving into temptation even more! Can you believe that? I mean, from God's perspective, do you have any idea how horrible that is? Well, just in case you can't, maybe this story will help you out.

"Several years ago, one evening a woman was driving home when she noticed a huge truck behind her that was driving uncomfortably close. So, she stepped on the gas to gain some distance from the truck, but when she sped up, the truck did too.

In fact, the faster she drove, the faster the truck did too. So now the lady starts getting scared so she exited the freeway. But the truck stayed with her.

Then the woman turned up a main street, hoping to lose her pursuer in traffic. But the truck ran a red light and continued the chase.

So now she's reaching the point of panic, so the woman whipped her car into a service station and bolted out of her car screaming for help.

And as she did this the driver of the truck sprang from his truck and ran toward her car. When he got there…he yanked the back door open and pulled out a man hidden in her back seat.

As it turned out, the woman was running from the wrong person!

From his high vantage point, the truck driver had spotted a would-be rapist in the woman's car. And thus, his chase wasn't to harm her but to save her even at the cost of his own safety."

Now, I don't know about you, but I bet when all was said and done, that lady was just a little bit glad that man chased her down, right? But now let's change the story a little bit. Now imagine that lady knew the rapist was in the back seat the whole time. But not only that, imagine she wanted the rapist there in her back seat. But not only that, imagine she refused to be rescued from the rapist. But not only that, imagine she did this day, after day, after day, after day? I mean, let's be honest. If she did that, we'd call her a "little crazy," right? How much crazier is it when we do that to God? How? By giving into temptation again, and again, when we don't have to? The fact is, God has rescued us! He's provided a way out! Yet, what do we do? We keep running into danger on purpose! Can you believe that? And from God's perspective, can you imagine how horrible that is? I mean, let's put it into its context. What if you went out of your way to rescue somebody day, after day, after day, from certain danger and they kept refusing your help? What would you do?

At some point wouldn't you say something like, "Well, fine! Have it your way! If you don't want my help, so be it. Get out of my face man! All I was doing was trying to help you out!" Right, isn't that what we would say? Then, how much more should God say that to you and me? But people, here's the good news. God isn't like you and me! He's faithful! And out of faithfulness, He not only forgives our sins, but He keeps on handing out His protection in spite of our sins! Can you believe that? Now that's what I call love, how about you?

The 3rd way the Bible reveals the faithfulness of God is that He keeps hearing our prayers.

Romans 12:11-12: "Never be lazy in your work but serve the Lord enthusiastically. Be glad for all God is planning for you. Be patient in trouble, and always be prayerful."

So here we see when it comes to the issue of daily prayers, the Bible not only says it's something good to do, but it's something that we should always do, right? What did the text say? It didn't say always think about prayer. It didn't say always read books on prayer. What did it say? It said to always be full of prayer, right? Why? Because stop and think about it. God didn't go through all this trouble of sending His One and Only Son, to die a gruesome death on the cross, and receive the punishment for all our sins, just to have a one-sided relationship. Are you kidding me? He said, "Cast all your cares upon Me." Because He cares, He wants to hear from us. Hebrews says what we have as a Christian, once we get saved, God, the creator of the universe, who's more exciting to talk to than Him! You've got direct access to His throne, the grace to approach His boldness in your time of need! I have a direct audience with God, and He wants to hear me! WOW! I'm running to that. I'm always going to be prayerful. What's more exciting than talking to God?

The Bible says Jesus endured the pain of the cross for the joy set before Him. And in case you didn't know that joy was the reality of having a two-sided relationship with you and me! And the point is this. You would think that someone who has freely been saved from eternal destruction in hell would naturally want to talk to God in prayer, right? But what do we see? Even though we know God wants us to talk to Him just like any other healthy relationship, what do we do? We talk to Him less than anyone else! Can you believe that? Well, in case you can't, I was able to find some proof. Let's take a look at what the average person does with their time if they live to the age of 75.

HOW WE SPEND OUR TIME

If we live 75 years, this is how we would spend it …

Activity	Percentage of time
23 years sleeping	31%
19 years working	25%
9 years watching TV or other amusements	12%
7.5 years in dressing and personal care	10%
6 years eating	8%
6 years traveling	8%
.5 year worshiping/praying	.07%

The Bible says we can grieve the Spirit of God! It hurts! When you marry somebody, you want to talk to them once in a while. And yet we talk to everybody else but Him. And to help drive this home we have another dog lesson. If you've got a cat, get it out of your head. It's not going to work. Dogs naturally want to spend time with you, they love you. At all times, it doesn't matter what is going on. But sometimes we kind of tease our dogs and they still want to hang out with us.

Dog owner: *"Food, I just couldn't stop thinking about it."*

Dog: *"Groan."*

Dog owner: *"So, I went to the fridge, and I opened up the meat drawer."*

Dog: *"Groan."*

Dog owner: *"You know what the meat drawer is, right?"*

Dog: *"Yes. What was in there?"* He groans.

Dog owner: *"I'll tell you what was in there. You know that bacon that tastes like maple flavor?"*

Dog: *"Maple kind, yeah."* He groans.

Dog owner: *"Well, I took that out and thought, I know who would like that. Me, so I ate it!"*

Dog: *"Oooooh! You're kidding me."* He groans.

Dog owner: *"Nope. I'm not kidding. And I noticed, there was some beef in there. You know, juicy steak, well, I ate that too!"*

Dog: *"Ooooooh!"* He groans.

Dog owner: *"Well, I went back to the fridge, just a few minutes ago, and I put something together, really special. You're going to love this one. I took some chicken, I put some cheese on it and I covered it with cat treats and guess what?"*

Dog: *"What?"* He groans.

Dog owner: *"I gave it to the cat."*

At that point the dog opens his mouth and yells out a big howl in disappointment.

That's right, we tease our dogs, but they don't get it. They just keep coming back because they want more. They just want to spend time with you. And that reminds me of a time during my first senior pastorate and I was fighting for time to study with all the interruptions. I finally found a place with some privacy where I could study. I closed the door and suddenly there is a scratching at the door. It was my female wiener dog. She knew I was in that room. I closed the door and she wanted near me. I thought, I can play that game; I'm just going to ignore it. But it didn't stop, it went on for five minutes. Then I'm thinking I'm going to have to repair the door, the scratch marks, I'm going to have to repaint the thing. I can't study. So, I get up, "You win!" So, I opened the door, picked her up and she just nestled in my side, and she was content.

And then I thought, is that God's attitude with spending time with us? He wants it so badly that He'll claw and scratch until the opportunity opens up, just to have time for you to spend with the Father. I felt so convicted that here is a dog that will claw and scratch just to spend time with me. She just wants to be with the master because she loves him. Like what this dog did with his master.

"At a hospital in Southwestern Siberia a loyal dog named Masha spent every day for two years, looking for her owner. Masha's owner

passed away last year after being taken to the hospital two years ago and ever since then the dog has shown up every day. Staff members at the hospital reportedly feed the dog and they make sure she has somewhere warm to sleep. One family wanted to adopt the dog, but she ran away, being back at the hospital hours later. When the owner was still alive and being treated at the hospital, Masha was his only visitor. One of the doctors at the hospital was quoted as saying, "You see her eyes, how sad they are – it's not the usual shiny eyes for when a dog is happy. You can see this in animals in the same way as with people."

Do we see that with people? Specifically with Christian people? Here's a dog showing up every day at the hospital, just to spend time with the master for two years, non-stop, not realizing that that's not ever going to happen again. But hoping every day that when it comes time to spend time with the Heavenly Master who rescued us from eternal damnation and hell. Maybe. Or do we make excuses? I don't know how to pray. I'll pray to God tomorrow.

Can you imagine what that must be in God's perspective. Imagine, you saved someone from certain death, as if it was your only child, and then the person you saved refused to talk to you. And then when you try to make conversation with them, they shrug it off. They don't know how to talk to you, they don't have time. Wouldn't you just like to say, "Get out of here you ungrateful wretch. I gave my child's life for you, to spend time with you, and you don't want anything to do with me." What would you do? Aren't you glad God is not like us? Aren't you glad for this aspect of His love? But here's the good news. God isn't like you and me! He's faithful! And out of faithfulness He not only forgives our sins, but He keeps on hearing our prayers, in spite of our sins! Can you believe that? I'll take that over the sicko twisted thing going on in the church.

The 7th way the Bible reveals that God is love is that God gives us goodness.

Psalm 69:13-18: "But I pray to you, O Lord, in the time of your favor; in your great love, O God answer me with your sure salvation. Rescue me from the mire, do not let me sink; deliver me from those who hate me, from the deep waters. Do not let the floodwaters engulf me or the depths swallow me up or the pit close its mouth over me, answer me, O Lord, out of the goodness of your love; in your great mercy turn to me. Do not hide your face from your servant; answer me quickly, for I am in trouble. Come near and rescue me; redeem me because of my foes."

So here we see when you and I are in times of trouble and we call out to God, what is the Psalmist confident that God will do? He will not only hear us, but what? He'll come near and rescue us, right? And why is the Psalmist so confident that God will do this? It is because we're so wonderful and we're so faithful to obey God? It is because we just have rotten things happening to us for no reason at all? No! Half of the problems in our life are caused by who? They are caused by us! Therefore, the Psalmist pleads for help, not on the basis of our behavior but on the basis of God's behavior, or in other words, out of the goodness of His love. And isn't it a great thing to know that God will help us, in spite of ourselves? Therefore, in order to better appreciate the love of God, I think we'd better take a closer look at the goodness of God and it's pretty simple.

The 1st way the Bible reveals the goodness of God is that He keeps on using us.

II Corinthians 4:5,7: "We don't go around preaching about ourselves; we preach Christ Jesus, the Lord. All we say about ourselves is that we are your servants because of what Jesus has done for us. But we have this treasure in jars of clay to show that this all – surpassing power is from God and not from us."

So, here we see when it comes to the issue of being used by God, the power to live for God comes from who? It comes from God, right? What did the text say? It says He stores His powerful treasure in jars of clay, or in other words, crackpots! And the reason why I say crackpots is because even though we're empowered by God to live for God, what do we do? We still sin, don't we? Therefore, our pots are cracked! You and I as Christians are nothing but a bunch of crackpots! Talk about the goodness of God. Instead of chucking us out in the back forty to rot and waste away, what does God do? He still uses our sinful crackpot lives for His glory. Isn't that amazing? But it's not only amazing, it's been His plan from the beginning. And to show you what I mean, let's take a look at the kind of people God used in the past.

HEROES OF THE FAITH

Moses stuttered.
David's armor didn't fit.
John Mark was rejected by Paul.
Hosea's wife was a prostitute.
Amos' only training was in fig tree pruning.
John was self-righteous.
Naomi was a widow.
Paul was a murderer. So was Moses.
Jonah ran from God.
Miriam was a gossip.
Jacob was a liar.
David had an affair.
Timothy had ulcers.
Peter was afraid of death.
Lazarus was dead.
Gideon and Thomas both doubted.
Jeremiah was depressed and suicidal.
Elijah was burned out.
John the Baptist was a loudmouth.
Martha was a worrywart.
Mary was lazy.
Samson had long hair.
Noah got drunk.

Now, I don't know about you, but I'd say that those people were just as big of crackpots as you and I are today. And the point is this. It's obvious that God doesn't use us because of our behavior, but He uses us in spite of our behavior, right? Isn't that good news? Well, it should be, but that's right. We've got a problem. You see, even though we know we're never going to be perfect, even as Christians, for some reason we still think God's only going to use us if we live perfect lives.

So, when we do blow it, and we will, we get tricked into thinking that God can't use us anymore! We've committed the unpardonable sin. We might as well stop serving God and go crawl in a hole and die! But think about it. If God were to wait for us to become perfect before He uses us, then what would happen? He'd still be waiting, right? And please don't misunderstand me. I am not saying we shouldn't be concerned about being obedient to God and try to refrain from a life of sin. Hello! The Bible says that if that's really your attitude then you might want to make sure you really got saved in the first place. But the point still remains. If the standard of behavior for God to use anyone was perfection…

He never would've used David because He had an affair.
He never would've used Noah because he got drunk.
He never would have used Moses or Paul because they were murderers!

And this is what's so amazing about the goodness of God. Every single one of us, as Christians, are going to blow it. But what does God do? Does He reject us? Does He refuse to use us ever again for His glory? Does He cast us away saying, "Get out of here! I never want to see your face again, you worthless piece of trash! I'm sick of your disobedience!" Is that what He does? No! He's not like you and I. God is Good! And out of His goodness, He not only saves us from our sins, but He keeps on using us, in spite of our sins! Can you believe that? Now that's what I call love, how about you?

Oh, but that's not all. The 2nd way the Bible reveals the goodness of God is that He keeps on blessing us.

Romans 8:28: "And we know that in all things God works for the good of those who love him, who have been called according to his purpose."

So, now we see, when it comes to the issue of being blessed by God or working all things together for good, who does God do it for? He does it for those who love Him. For His children, right? But notice what the text did not say. It didn't say He'd work out some things in your life for good. It didn't say He'd work out most things for good. What did it say? It said He'd work out <u>all</u> things for good!

But that's still not all. Neither did the text say God would only work out all things for good who lived perfect lives, did it? No! Therefore, that means God doesn't bless us because of our behavior, but in spite of our behavior, right? And isn't that good news? Well, it should be, but that's right. We've got a problem. Even though God demonstrates this truth again and again in our lives, we still don't believe Him! And because of this we needlessly get all worked up in fear and worry when the whole time we don't have to! Why? Because there's plenty of evidence of the goodness of God all around us.

For instance, remember the story of when Brandie and I were $4,000 in the hole overnight? We had no idea what we were going to do. But when all was said and done it all worked together for good because God put it on the heart of a non-Christian to give us a gift of $5,000, which meant we just made $1,000 bucks. Now granted, that was a rough way to make $1,000 bucks but hey, I'm glad it worked out the way it did. Or the time when I got ditched by co-workers in Chicago and had to make a mad dash to the airport? When all was said and done it all worked together for good because I ended up changing seats and sitting next to Dr. Desmond Ford who proceeded for the next couple of hours to convince me to go back to school and do my graduate studies.

Which meant that I resigned from my current Pastorate and took a sabbatical to go to seminary, which led me to take on another Pastorate where unbeknownst to me God birthed a media ministry... Which led to a full-time global teaching ministry which led to getting a phone call one day from a guy in Las Vegas saying their Church wanted to talk to me. Which led to me taking that position where now the Gospel is going out to 218 countries worldwide!

I don't know about you, but I'm glad that those people ditched me in Chicago, you know what I'm saying? And here's the point. I'd say God's really working all things together for good, how about you? The problem is not in the goodness of God, it's our lack of trust in the goodness of God! And therefore, we don't need to get all worked up in fear and worry, no matter how bad the circumstances might be, like the people of Wedgwood Baptist Church learned.

How many of you remember several years back about the tragedy at Wedgwood Baptist Church? You know, where that gunman entered the sanctuary and killed 7 people and injured 7 others before killing himself? Well, could God really work even that horrible instance together for good? Well, let's find out. Let's take a look at the rest of the story.

ALL THINGS FOR GOOD?

"Before the shooting, the Pastor prayed that God would do whatever it took to expand the ministry of Wedgwood Baptist Church. To enter the Church sanctuary the gunman walked past the children's playground, which should have been full of kids, but for some reason every single children's and preschool class was running late so no one had made it to the playground yet.

The gunman fired over 100 bullets into a crowd of over 400, but only 14 people were hit and he did not shoot over 60 bullets he still had with him. The bottom fell off of a pipe bomb he threw, and the bomb landed without ever exploding.

One of the youth that was wounded (she was shielding a disabled friend with her body) had scoliosis. Therefore the curve in her spine directed the bullet away from major organs, saving her from serious injury.

One of the people in the sanctuary at that time was a paramedic, and he was able to stop bleeding and stabilize injured people before the emergency crews arrived.

None of the adults who died had children. All 7 victims were not just Christians, but bold Christians who were passionate about their faith.

Many members at Wedgwood Baptist are healing broken relationships within the body and experiencing spiritual renewal. At several schools, students met around their flagpoles the next day. At one school 25 students accepted Christ, and 110 at another. A teacher led 22 students to Christ in her classroom.

The Pastor presented the gospel on Larry King Live when prompted by a question asked by Al Gore.

Every time the gunman fired a bullet, he intended to take a life. But God turned that around and saved several lives for each bullet fired. The faith of those who died has been multiplied many times over.

CNN broadcasted the memorial service live. Amazingly, because one of the victim's families lives and works in Saudi Arabia, that country allowed the service to be broadcast there as well.

In Saudi Arabia it is illegal to say the name of Jesus on the street. And because of that same CNN broadcast, 35 people in Japan gave their lives to Christ.

They immediately received over 70,000 hits on their web page, which displays the plan of salvation in multiple languages.

Because of the live news coverage and interviews, over 200 million people have heard the gospel because of this tragedy."

Now, I don't know about you, but I'd say God really can work all things together for good, you know what I'm saying? And the point is this. Remember the context in which God does this. Most of these problems that God keeps turning around for good are caused by who? They're not caused by a gunmen bent on destruction. They're caused by our own destruction. Our own sinful behavior!

Therefore, what does God do? Does He reject us? Does He refuse to ever bless us again? Does He cast us away saying, "I'm so sick and tired of fixing all your problems that you keep creating yourself. Get out of here!" Is that what he does? No! He's not like you and I. God is good! And out of goodness He not only saves us from our sins, but He keeps on blessing us, in spite of our sins! Can you believe that? Now that's what I call love, how about you?

Oh, but that's not all. The 3rd way the Bible reveals the Goodness of God is that He keeps on loving us. Did you know that God loves you just as much today as He did when you first cried out to receive Christ as your savior? It never wanes, it never lessens, in fact He promised that it will never go away.

Hebrews 13:5: "Because God has said, 'Never will I leave you; Never will I forsake you."

So, now we see when it comes to the issue of being loved by God, what did the text say? Did it say God will stay with you as long as you remain that perfect person? Did it say He's going to leave and forsake you the very first time you blow it? No! What did it say? It said He'd never leave you nor forsake you, right? In fact, in the original Greek, it's much more emphatic. Let's look at it.

Hebrews 13:5: "For He himself has said, and the statement is on record, I will not, I will not cease to sustain and uphold you. I will not, I will not, I will not let you down."

And basically, this passage is kind of like God's way of saying, "Listen up! If you belong to Me, you've got to get this through your heads. You belong to Me forever! I'm not ever going to leave you!" And what makes this so amazing is the context in which God makes this promise. Keep in mind… This is the same God who has shown us mercy by giving us a palace in Heaven instead of a pit in hell, a body of perfection instead of a body of pain and a heavenly greeting instead of a hellish goodbye.

And then if that wasn't enough, He shows us compassion by dying for those who wanted Him dead and continually forgiving our continual sins. And then if that wasn't enough, He shows us kindness by accepting sinners just as they are, He turns them into saints, and then He turns them into sons. And then if that wasn't enough, He shows us graciousness by giving us the grace to obey, serve, and love Him even after we're saved! And then if that wasn't enough, He shows us patience by not only putting up with our sins until we get saved, but He puts up with our sins even after we're saved! And then if that wasn't enough, He shows us faithfulness by providing, protecting, and hearing our prayers in spite of our sins! And the point is this. Even after all this love God's given to us, what do we do? We sin against Him, don't we?

Therefore, what does He do? Does He reject us? Does He refuse to love us ever again? Does He cast us away saying, "I have had it up to here with you! After all I've done for you, you still keep sticking the knife in my back! Get out of here you wretch!" Is that what He does? No! He's not like you and I. God is Good! And out of goodness He not only saves us from our sins, but He keeps on loving us, in spite of our sins! Can you believe that? What did the verse say? I will never leave you nor forsake you, right? It's God's way of saying, "Listen up! If you belong to Me, you've got to get this through your heads… No matter what you do, no matter what you've done, you belong to Me forever! I'm not going to leave you!"

I (God) your Heavenly Father, will make sure you make it across the finish line to Heaven, like this Father did with his son…

"With music playing in the background, "My Redeemer Lives," you see a dad pushing his son in a wheelchair. He takes him out on the pavement, running as fast as he can. The son looks like he may be in his early twenties and is very disabled. As the video progresses, you realize that they are in a competition against others. There are several steps that they go through. One is crossing a body of water in a raft, the dad swims while pulling his son in the raft. When they get to shore the dad picks up his son and carries him to the next test. He is put into a chair fastened to a bicycle

and the dad peddles his son to the next test. When you look at the son's face, he has the biggest smile. He is loving every minute of this competition. Of course, dad is a little tired. The son is again put into his chair and the dad is now running and pushing him to the finish line. It is now dark. They have been doing this all day and all the other competitors have completed the race and they are all just waiting for the dad and his son to come to the finish line. They finally reach the finish line, everyone cheers, a standing ovation. The son is so happy, he is waving his arms with a great big smile on his face. Even though he was unable to do this on his own, his dad brought him across the finish line."

"I can do all things through Him who strengthens me." **Philippians 4:13**

Because my Redeemer lives, I can do all things through Him Who strengthens me, including making it across the finish line called Heaven. That's what God does for us every day. How do you know you're getting there? He's going to complete the work. With all of our debilitations, with all the sins we get involved in, sometimes it feels like you can't walk anymore. Sometimes you are so beat up you can hardly even crawl. You know what God will do? He's going to complete the work.

That was retired Lieutenant Colonel Dick Hoyt in the military for 37 years who is pushing his son Rick a quadriplegic in an Iron Man Competition because he told his dad, "Dad, when I'm running, it feels like I'm not handicapped."

They've now finished over 1,000 races and they finish every time, so his son could feel the victory. And here's my point. God, through Jesus Christ, not only forgives you of all your sins, and heals you of all your brokenness, but even if we become debilitated by sin again, where it's affecting our walk, we're still making it to Heaven. Why? Because like that earthly father, our Heavenly Father is the One pushing us to the finish line, and He never loses! He always makes it across the finish line! He will complete the good work he began in you! He'll get you there!

I'll take that as Biblical love over the twisted sick perverted version that is rampant in the church today. Because we now have enemies within the church destroying things. Including the lie of homosexuality and transgenderism and gender fluidity.

Chapter Six

The Twisting of Biblical Relationships

So far, we've seen how the enemies, fakers, have invaded the church through our seminaries, Bible colleges, and denominations and their perversion and twisting of God's truth and His Biblical love. They say it's eros instead of agapao. So that's why they say we should allow any and all sinful behavior. But what is His Biblical love? So far, we've seen God reveals He is love by...

Giving us mercy. He gives His enemies a palace in Heaven instead of a pit in hell, a body of perfection instead of a body of pain and a Heavenly greeting instead of a hellish goodbye.

Showing us compassion, by dying for those who wanted Him dead, but He continually forgives our continual sins.

Gives us kindness, by accepting sinners just as they are, He turns them into saints and then He turns them into sons.

Gives us graciousness, by giving us the grace not only to get saved, but He gives us the grace to obey, serve, and love Him even after we're saved!

Shows us patience, by not only putting up with our sins until we get saved, but He puts up with our sins even after we're saved!

Gives us faithfulness, by not only saving us from our sins, but He keeps on providing, protecting, and hearing our prayers, in spite of our sins!

And then finally, He gives us goodness by not only saving us from our sins, but He keeps on using us, blessing us, and loving us, in spite of our sins! Isn't that incredible?

I'll take that love over the sick, twisted, perverted one today. That leads us to the next act of perversion. They've not only twisted the Biblical definition of love … they've done the same thing with God's promise of the rainbow! You do recall the Biblical definition of the rainbow, right? You know, the promise from God that He will never destroy the whole world again because of sin, with a flood? A worldwide flood that is, because local floods still do happen. That's not what God's talking about. I mentioned that for the skeptics. But God used the rainbow as a sign that He would never bring a global flood, to bring a global judgment to our planet because of sin.

However, that does not mean that He's not going to judge the planet again because of sin. Rather we know He is, but this time by fire! I didn't say that He did!

2 Peter 3:10: "But the Day of the Lord will come like a thief. The heavens will disappear with a roar; the elements will be destroyed by fire, and the earth and everything in it will be laid bare."

God is clearly going to judge the planet again for sin, with fire this time, because man just doesn't seem to stop! In fact, it goes on to say, here's the logical response of how you should live, if you knew this was coming!

2 Peter 3:11: "Since everything will be destroyed in this way what kind of people ought you to be? You ought to live holy and godly lives."

Why? God's watching all this. You can't hide anything from Him, let alone your sin. Instead, receive His mercy and forgiveness through Jesus Christ and show your gratefulness by living holy and godly lives, right? Common sense! Unfortunately, that's not what's happening today! The rainbow has not only been hijacked and twisted from its original meaning to celebrate sin, but in light of the Supreme Court decision, the White House actually projected a twisted meaning of the rainbow on its very premises! Flaunting it in God's face! You talk about audacity! Remember this?

Now I don't know about you, that's not only blasphemous, but God's people can't be pleased with this, can we agree? I mean, can you imagine the audacity of this? Our Nation is headed for judgment unless we turn around real fast, amen? In fact, I'm not the only one saying this. So is this guy!

Franklin Graham: *"Obama had the White House lit up in rainbow colors to celebrate the Supreme Court ruling on same-sex marriage. This* *is outrageous – a real slap in the face to the millions of Americans who do not support same-sex marriage and whose voice is being ignored.*

God is the one who gave the rainbow, and it was associated with His judgment. God sent a flood to wipe out the entire world because mankind had become so wicked and violent.

One man, Noah, was found righteous and escaped God's judgment with his family. The rainbow was a sign to Noah that God would not use the flood again to judge the world.

But one day God is going to judge sin – all sin. Only those who are found righteous will be able to escape His judgment.

That righteousness comes through faith, believing on the Name of the Lord Jesus Christ who took our sins and shed His blood on the cross for each and every one.

So, when we see the gay pride rainbow splashed on business advertisements and many people's Facebook pages, may it remind all of us of God's judgment to come. Are you ready? Are your sins forgiven?"

So, that's the point! Have you accepted Jesus Christ as your Lord and Savior, have you asked Him to forgive you of your sins, and turned from sins yourself or are you still celebrating sin even in the Church with the rest of the world? Are you going to be swallowed up in the next coming judgment?

Which is why we're going to take a look at, "A Biblical View of Homosexuality." And believe it or not, as a nation we have opened up Pandora's Box with this decision to support same-sex marriage, and it's the worst thing you could ever do. You think it's bad now? You ain't seen nothing yet! I didn't say that. God did.

Romans 1:18-32: "The wrath of God is being revealed from Heaven against all the godlessness and wickedness of men who suppress the truth by their wickedness, since what may be known about God is plain to them, because God has made it plain to them. For since the creation of the world God's invisible qualities – his eternal power and divine nature – have been clearly seen, being understood from what has been made, so that men are without excuse. For although they knew God, they neither glorified him as God nor gave thanks to him, but their thinking became futile, and their foolish hearts were darkened. Although they claimed to be wise, they became fools and exchanged the glory of the immortal God for images made to look like mortal man and birds and animals and reptiles. Therefore, God gave them over in the sinful desires of their hearts to sexual impurity for the degrading of their bodies with one another. They exchanged the truth of God for a lie and worshiped and served created things rather than the Creator – who is forever praised. Amen. Because of this, God gave them over to shameful lusts. Even their women exchanged natural relations for unnatural ones. In the same way the men also abandoned natural relations with women and were inflamed with lust for one another. Men committed indecent acts with other men and received in themselves the due penalty for their perversion."

This is not acceptable by God. You may choose that as a lifestyle, but it's sin! It's not just a sin, it's called a perversion that is against God's design. Against His relationship. Like it, lump it, believe it or not, God is our Creator, we're created in His image as male and female. When you are married, it's man and woman. That's it, anything else is a perversion. I didn't say it, He did. But here's my point. Notice the timing. You've got the 50s and 60s, here comes evolution, right after that God gives you over to free love, free sex, and that goes into the 60s and 70s. What happened in the 80s? Here comes Rock Hudson and AIDS. Here comes all the sympathy for these people, and then in the 80s and 90s you have homosexuality and lesbians being accepted. Even in the church. Now, did we turn away from that? No! And now we are here where we are at.

Romans 1:18-32, cont.: "Furthermore, since they did not think it worthwhile to retain the knowledge of God, he gave them over to a depraved mind, to do what ought not to be done."

I'm telling you, in the news you need to translate. Don't just use the words, that's insane, how could they say that they don't know what a woman is? Hey, that's just ridiculous, I mean what kind of a comment is that, that you would actually approve that, and teach that to kids? What do you mean, that you're having a drag queen read stories to kids? It's not just that it's unbelievable, what's the Biblical term? That's a depraved mind! You're watching a depraved mind in action. You try to talk and it's like you're talking to a brick wall. I don't even know how to respond. That's not just wrong, it's a depraved mind. It's what God said would happen when you don't turn away from your error. Once you lied about evolution, said he didn't exist, but He gave you plenty of evidence, He handed over your sexual morality, you just turned away from that, now you are going into homosexuality and lesbianism and here's where we're at today.

Romans 1:18-32 cont.: "They have become filled with every kind of wickedness, evil, greed and depravity. They are full of envy, murder, strife, deceit, and malice. They are gossips, slanderers, God-haters, insolent, arrogant and boastful; they invent ways of doing evil; they disobey their parents; they are senseless, faithless, heartless, ruthless. Although they know God's righteous decree that those who do such things deserve death, they not only continue to do these very things but also approve of those who practice them."

You know, they start passing laws in every state to force you to go into this! It's the exact same thing God said was going to happen! If you ever wanted to know why America is going down the tubes so fast, here it is. We're following the same path the Roman society did. They first turned to an evolutionary mindset that said there was no God, even though there is plenty of evidence for God's existence through His creation. So, what did God do? God gave them over to shameful lusts. And that was with homosexuality and lesbianism. And then what happened after that? They still refused to retain the knowledge of God. Now things got really dark. God gave them over to a depraved mind to do what ought not to be done.

Evil, greed, slander, murder, strife, gossip, God-hating people who actually invented ways of doing evil and then even approved of those who are doing such things! Now does that sound familiar or what? That's America! That's what's wrong with us! We're following the same path of the Roman Society and we're reaping the same destruction…even in the Church! Which mean we're under the wrath of God just like they were! It's opened up Pandora's Box. And we're getting worse by the day, just like God said it would! Once you go down this route of approving homosexuality it will open the doors to absolutely unimaginable behavior! Don't believe me? It's already begun…

Opening Pandora's/Satan's Box

It's Complicated‡

All this ongoing redefinition of marriage with same sex unions is now including the idea of what's being called, "non-monogamy"…

God calls it polygamy, right? But now it's okay because it's non-monogamy.

Opening Pandora's/Satan's Box

Or in other words, the acceptance of "multiple partners" or literally "polygamy" without the stigma of adultery. In fact, it's already being pushed in light of the Supreme Court's Ruling...

Right after the Supreme Court decision, immediately began to open up Pandora's box.

EQUALITY FOR ALL?

POLYGAMIST WANTS MARRIAGE AFTER SAME-SEX RULING

NEWSROOM

CNN Reports: *"My next guest is a polygamist. He's already legally married to one woman and now he would like to marry a second saying the basis for this past Supreme Court ruling for same-sex couples is about* *inclusion and legal legitimacy for all consenting adults. So, why not for polygamists as well. He says this is his argument."*

Field Reporter: *"Nathan Collier and his partner Christine went to the Yellowstone County courthouse looking to be wed under the marriage equality act. The Colliers practiced polygamy but it's currently illegal under Montana state law."*

Nathan Collier: *"We just want to add legal legitimacy to an already happy, functional, strong, loving family."*

Field Reporter: *"As the two filled out their marriage application, they were met with questions."*

Clerk: *"You are married to someone else?"*

Nathan Collier: *"Yes, I am married to my first wife, Victoria."*

Field Reporter: *"The couple was met with surprise."*

Typist: *"So, are you legally married?"*

Nathan Collier: *"I'm legally married to Victoria."*

Typist: *"You didn't get a divorce from her yet?"*

Nathan Collier: *"No, we're a plural family. I'm a polygamist. We're not even asking for acceptance. We're just asking for tolerance."*

Field Reporter: *"The Colliers say if the state of Montana could recognize their marriage as legal, it could be the catalyst for other states to follow suit."*

You mess with God's design; He's going to give you over to a depraved mind! You start doing things that ought not to be done. That happened the very next day. Already starting to push it. You opened

Pandora's Box and again that's why I think it was a spiritual moment for our country. Not a good one either! You just opened up the floodgates of destruction. So, now let's fast forward to today. And not only the catalyst of other states following suit but the catalyst for even more bizarre redefinitions of sexuality & marriage!
It's now called Gender Fluidity.

What's that? What is Gender Fluidity? God created male and female, but now we don't know what a woman is. And polygamy. That word still has a little bit of a sting. That probably isn't good behavior. Let's just call it non-monogamy. That's all they've done; it's just word speak. Just because you change the definition of sin, doesn't make it not sin. But that is what the world does. They take what God calls sin and they just change the term and then they force this to be acceptable behavior. But gender fluidity is crazy. I was watching an interview where they were saying even babies, not even toddlers or adolescents, may have questions about their gender. A baby! You know what that is? That's what is called a depraved mind! This is insane, I'm convinced that our country, right now, is being led by half of the church that thinks this is okay. They are being led by depraved minds!

It's not just unbiblical, it's not just insane and dumb, it's a depraved mind! And it just keeps getting worse because we're either complicit, or we keep our mouth shut on it, and that doesn't help anything. It certainly doesn't help these kids. And as we learned in our Satanist study, half of all Satanists are homosexuals. That's their statistics. And that's because the number one law of satanism is what? Do what you will, shall be the whole of the law. Whatever you want to do, total rebellion, I will be with whoever I want to be with, I don't care what God says. So now we have gender fluidity, and we have all their terms. God says male and female, there are only two. Here are just 46 terms and they just keep growing by the month. We have gone from male and female to this:

46 Terms That Describe Sexual Attraction, Behavior, and Orientation

"Sexuality can be fluid — changing in different situations for some, and over the years for others.

Observing patterns in sexual and romantic attraction, behavior, and preferences over time is one way to better understand your sexual identity or romantic orientation."

Allosexual
A word describing those who experience sexual attraction and those who aren't part of the asexual community.

Allosexism
All should experience sexual attraction.

Androsexual
Those who have a sexual or romantic attraction to men, males, or masculinity.

Asexual
No sexual attraction to others of any gender.

Aromantic

People who have little or no romantic attraction, regardless of sex or gender.

Autosexual
A person who's sexually attracted to themselves.

Autoromantic
A person who's romantically attracted to themselves.

Bicurious
People who are exploring bisexuality.

Bisexual
People who experience sexual attractions to people of more than one gender.

Biromantic
Those who experience romantic attraction of more than one gender.

Closeted
Closeted, also referred to as "in the closet," describes people in the LGBTQIA+ community who don't publicly or openly share their sexual identity, sexual attraction, sexual behavior, gender expression, or gender identity.

Coming out
Those who are open about one's sexuality and gender.

Cupiosexual
Describes asexual people who don't experience sexual attraction but still have the desire to engage in sexual behavior or a sexual relationship.

Demisexual
Describes individuals who experience sexual attraction only under specific circumstances.

Demiromantic
Describes individuals who experience romantic attraction only under specific circumstances.

Fluid
The term to describe how sexuality, sexual attraction, and sexual behavior can change over time and be dependent on the situation.

Gay
Those who are attracted to the same gender.

Graysexual
A term used to acknowledge the gray area on the sexuality spectrum.

Grayromantic
A person whose gray area is between romantic and aromantic.

Gynesexual
Those who have a sexual or romantic attraction to women, females, or femininity.

Heterosexual
Those who have a sexual, romantic, or emotional attraction to people of the "opposite" gender (i.e., male vs. female, man vs. woman). Commonly described as straight.

Homosexual
People attracted to the same gender.

Lesbian
A woman attracted to the same gender
.

Libidoist asexual
A term used to describe an asexual person who experiences sexual feelings that are satisfied through self-stimulation.

Monosexual
Those who are exclusively heterosexual, gay, or lesbian.

Non-libidoist asexual
Someone who doesn't experience any sexual feelings or have an active sex drive.

Omnisexual
Omnisexual is similar to pansexual describing individuals whose sexuality isn't limited to people of a particular gender, sex, or sexual orientation.

Pansexual
A term that describes individuals who can experience sexual, or romantic, or attraction to any person, regardless of that person's gender, sex, or sexuality.

Panromantic
Those who have a romantic, (but not sexual) attraction to any person, regardless of that person's gender, sex, or sexuality.

Polysexual
Those who have a sexual or romantic attraction to people with varying genders

Pomosexual
Those who reject sexual labels or don't identify with any of them.

Passing
Passing refers to those who pass on society's perceptions and assumptions of someone's sexuality or gender.

Queer
An umbrella term that describes individuals who aren't exclusively heterosexual.

Questioning

The process of being curious about or exploring some aspect of sexuality or gender.

Romantic attraction
The experience of having an emotional response that results in the desire for a romantic, but not necessarily sexual, relationship or interaction with another person or oneself.

Romantic orientation
Is an aspect of self and identity that involves how you experience romantic desire (if you do).

Sapiosexual
Those who experience attraction based on intelligence, rather than sex or gender.

Sexual attraction
Those who have a sexual desire to another person or group of people.

Sex-averse
Those who are asexual and are averse to any sex or sexual behavior.

Sex-favorable
The "opposite" of sex repulsed.

Sex-indifferent
Those who are indifferent or neutral about sex or sexual behavior.

Sexual orientation or sexuality
Describing how you feel or experience sexual or romantic desire (if you do).

Sex-repulsed
Those who are repulsed by in sex or sexual behavior.

Skoliosexual

Those who are attracted to people nonbinary, genderqueer, or trans.

Spectrasexual
Those who are attracted to multiple or varied sexes, genders, and gender identities — but not necessarily all or any.

Straight
Also known as heterosexual, (Also known as God's way!)

You know who came out with this list? A depraved mind! Isn't this nuts?! God says this when it comes to sexes.

Genesis 1:26-27: "Then God said, 'Let us make man in our image, in our likeness, and let them rule over the fish of the sea and the birds of the air, over the livestock, over all the earth, and over all the creatures that move along the ground.' So, God created man in His own image, in the image of God He created him; male and female He created them."

Pretty simple! But now you've been given over to a depraved mind! But it gets even worse just like God said! Now this redefinition of sexuality has given rise the even more bizarre redefinitions of marriage... not just homosexuality and polygamy ... But now people are getting married to their zombie dolls, the ocean, chandeliers, and a 300-year-old ghost pirate!

Woman in blue: *"Kelly, let's watch our wedding video."* She proceeds to put the DVD into the player and the ceremony is playing. The ceremony seems to have three humans attending. That would be the minister, the witness, and the bride. The bride is all dressed in white like a traditional bride but the groom she is kissing is a zombie doll. And if you look at the guests attending the ceremony, they are also zombie dolls. They are in all shapes and sizes. Two of them are dressed in white also as her bridesmaids. When the video is over, and we are back in her living room she is sitting on the couch with her groom. She has her arm around him, reliving the ceremony.

Woman in blue: *"That was such a special day. I really love you and I really enjoyed marrying you. I can't wait to spend the rest of my life with you."* And she gives him a big kiss on the cheek.

The next video is of several people at the beach. They aren't there to swim.

Leader: *"We're going to do a welcome to start but just keep in mind that we're going to go around and any vows that you want to make to the sea or to water, you'll have a chance to speak your vows or a poem or give them a flower or whatever you want to do, or you can stay silent and just pass."*

First speaker: *"Today we stand upon this holy earth and in this sacred space to witness the rite of matrimony between the sea and us all."*

The next video is of a woman kissing her chandelier.

Amanda Liberty: *"Hello, I'm in love with chandeliers and I'm making a commitment to my favorite one, Lumiere. I love you."* She is humming as she is kissing it again.

The final video is of a woman who married a ghost pirate.

"My name is Amanda Sparrow Large Tee, I'm a witch, I'm a spiritual teacher and I'm well known for marrying the ghost of a 300-year-old pirate."

Narrator: *"So, how did you guys meet?"*

Amanda: *"Well, how we first met was while I was in my room, I felt this energy around me. It was unfamiliar to me. It was not one of the energies I was used to working with. So, at that point I said clearly, this energy, this entity wants to connect with me, that it has something that it wants to say. So, I decided that I would communicate."*

Narrator: *"What did he tell you about himself?"*

Amanda: *"The first thing he said to me was, I'm dead you know, and I said yes, I do get that. I asked him obviously who he was and what his purpose was. He told me that his name was Jack Teague and that he was a pirate."*

No, actually he's a demon, a familiar spirit! You just married a demon! Why? Because you've been given over to a depraved mind! And this isn't even counting the people who married,

The Eiffel Tower
The Berlin Wall
A Tree
A Bear
A Bridge
Married Themselves
Then Cheating on Themselves
Then Divorced Themselves

Who does that? And just as God warned, once you go down this route, you just opened up Pandora's Box.

You deny God – Evolution
You accept Homosexuality & Lesbianism
You will start doing things that ought not to be done!
And just like God warned it gets even worse!

You now start accepting pedophilia.

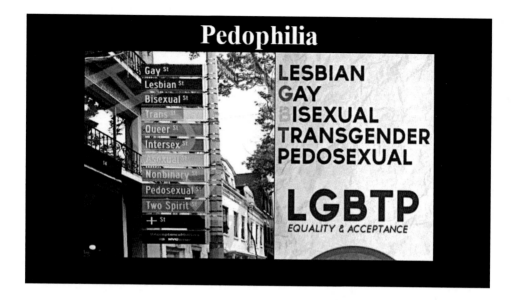

I deliberately show that picture because, notice how that little acronym keeps getting bigger and longer. And look at what's down there right below non-binary, the new term, pedosexual. Pedophilia. Homosexual, pedosexual, what's the difference? That's their choice, right? This is exactly what is happening. God warned about this, and He also says this is not acceptable behavior. God says…

Romans 1:31: "They are senseless, faithless, heartless (*without natural affection*), ruthless."

2 Timothy 3:1-3: "But mark this: There will be terrible times in the last days. People will be lovers of themselves, lovers of money, boastful, proud, abusive, disobedient to their parents, ungrateful, unholy, without love, (*without natural affection*)."

Pedophiles share the characteristic of being "without natural affection" as mentioned in Romans 1:31; 2 Timothy 3:2.

The phrase "without natural affection" is translated from one Greek word, "astorgos" which means "inhuman, unloving, and unsociable." One without natural affection acts in ways that are against the social norm. This would certainly describe a pedophile. And those people who do these things will not inherit the kingdom of God.

1 Corinthians 6:9-10: "Do you not know that the wicked will not inherit the kingdom of God? Do not be deceived: Neither the sexually immoral nor idolaters nor adulterers nor *male prostitutes* nor homosexuals nor thieves nor the greedy nor drunkards nor slanderers nor swindlers will inherit the kingdom of God."

"Male prostitutes" or "effeminate" is the Greek word "malakos" which refers to a "catamite" or "a boy kept for homosexual relations with a man."

A Catamite was a term used, "In ancient Greece and Rome, a catamite was a pubescent boy who was the intimate companion of a man, usually in a pedophile relationship."

So, there you go! God says...don't do that...pedophilia! You won't inherit the Kingdom of God! But since we've rejected God's definition of marriage and twisted Biblical love, now apparently, we can make it up as you go!

Not only be who you want to be but be with whoever you want to be with! That's a lifestyle they choose. Who cares what God says and do it anyway in rebellion. Well, did we speak up in the beginning with the reversal of traditional marriage? Did we speak up on homosexuality and lesbianism? And then here comes the polygamy and transgenderism, and we are dealing with "don't know what a woman is." Half the church is not speaking up and the other half, you may be Biblical, but when was the last time you taught on this? When is it ever talked about? When is that verse ever even quoted, that these people do not inherit the Kingdom of God? All this stuff is completely avoided. But again, God says, it's going to get worse. And believe it or not, that too is being promoted.

OPENING PANDORA'S/SATAN'S BOX

Judge Richard Posner, Federal judge with the 7th Circuit Court of Appeals and a supporter of the gay marriage movement says: *"Perhaps it's time the government begin issuing 'rape licenses' since the 'right to rape' for some men at least, 'exceeds the victim's physical and emotional pain.'"*

Now who says that? It's a depraved mind! So, in other words… once you redefine marriage, anything goes! Including pedophilia! In fact, laws are being changed to accommodate it and politicians are admitting that's who they are!"

Other legal officials are now saying that even pedophiles should have civil rights as. **Margo Kaplan, a Law Professor at Rutgers University** said this: *"People who are sexually attracted to children, must hide their disorder from everyone they know, or risk losing educational and job opportunities. So, the nation's anti-pedophilia laws are unfair to pedophiles and should be changed."*

Another judge in Australia said, *"Pedophilia and incest may no longer be considered taboo, just as gay relationships are now being more accepted than they used to be in the 50s and 60s."*

You've got to be kidding me! And now in the United States of America, in certain states, laws are actually being changed, not just to accommodate homosexuality, lesbianism, transgenderism, but even pedophilia. And now they are even running for office. And they admit it!

KLAS News reports: *"A new bill, SB-145, it's getting a lot of negative attention from people on both sides of the aisle. SB-145 would lower penalties for adults convicted of sex crimes with minors. Joining us to talk a little bit more about this is California State Senator Shannon Grove. Senator, thank you for talking to us tonight."*

Shannon Grove: *"Absolutely Ginger and thank you very much for the invitation to discuss this important issue."*

KLAS New reports: *"This bill was created by Senator Scott Weiner in San Francisco. Can you explain to us or give us an example of how it would work?"*

Shannon Grove: *"I mean we are going to have a frank conversation about this bill because this bill does affect our children. SB-145 would remove the requirement for offenders to register as sex offenders if they were committing certain sex crimes with minors and there was a 10-year age limit. The crimes that are excluded that make this bill even more detrimental are non-forcible oral copulation, non-forcible sodomy and non-forcible sexual penetration by a foreign object. So, let's just talk about that for a second. A fourteen-year-old being brought into a situation where she or he endures this type of act and then the perpetrator says, well it was voluntary, or they wanted to."*

The Young Turks reports: *"A congressional candidate from the state of Virginia has openly admitted that he was running a website that supported the notion of legalizing pedophilia, raping wives, and all sorts of things that you wouldn't imagine someone would publicly support. His name is Nathan Larson, and I am going to give you some of the details of what he included, of what he himself contributed to these websites. When asked if he is a pedophile or just writes about pedophilia. He said, 'It's a mix of both. When people go over the top there's a grain of truth to what they say.'"*

Next News Network: *"Legalizing sexual child abuse, yes, pedophilia is now classified as a sexual orientation. Hard to believe. Truth in Action News is reporting the unthinkable. They write that this would seem to be the very first step in tolerating the sodomizing of children. Pedophilia is now officially classified as a sexual orientation under the politically correct term 'minor attracted person.' Apparently, now people can classify themselves as heterosexual, homosexual, asexual, metrosexual, and then there are endless sexual orientations under the sun and now pedophilia can be added to the list."*

In other words, you rejected God with the lie of evolution, he handed you over to sexual immorality, you didn't turn from that, then he handed you over again, and you went to homosexuality, lesbianism and you wouldn't turn from that and now we're in that state of a depraved mind! And you are certainly doing things that ought not be done. How else would you describe something where you're passing laws so that people don't have to go to jail for committing pedophilia. Who does that? A nation in the last days of destruction. And nobody's talking about this. And just like God warned it's about to get even worse! The next thing you start to accept is bestiality.

Now bestiality still has a negative term to it. Kind of like polygamy. If you call polygamy, non-monogamy, I guess it's okay. Or plural family. Well, believe it or not, this is their new term to describe bestiality. Zoophilia. You know, it's just zoophilia. Or zoosexual. Those that identify as having sex with animals. No! It's bestiality! And God says this about it.

Exodus 22:19: "Anyone who has sexual relations with an animal must be put to death."

Leviticus 18:23-25: "Do not have sexual relations with an animal and defile yourself with it. A woman must not present herself to an animal to have sexual relations with it; that is a perversion. Do not defile yourselves in any of these ways, because this is how the nations that I am going to drive out before you became defiled. Even the land was defiled; so, I punished it for its sin, and the land vomited out its inhabitants."

Leviticus 20:15-16: "If a man has sexual relations with an animal, he must be put to death, and you must kill the animal. If a woman approaches an animal to have sexual relations with it, kill both the woman and the animal. They must be put to death; their blood will be on their own heads."

Deuteronomy 27:21: "Cursed is the man who has sexual relations with any animal. Then all the people shall say, 'Amen!'"

But we are now being governed by people who now have a depraved mind. They saw zoosexuality as a valid sexuality. But since we've rejected God's definition of marriage and sexuality apparently, we can make it up as you go!

Be who you want to be and be with whoever you want to be with, including an animal! This is from an article entitled…

ZOOSEXUALITY IS A VALID SEXUALITY

"Now, this is weird, trust me I know, but I've thought a lot about it and can't seem to see what everyone's problem with zoosexuals is."

"Some may call it repulsive but that's not a good enough reason to prevent someone from exploring whatever sexual interest they have with animals."

One congressman from Texas stated that, *"Gay marriage would be a slippery slope to polygamy and bestiality. When you say it's not a man and a woman anymore, then why not have three men and one woman or four women and one man? Or why not, you know, somebody has a love for an animal?"*

Whoa! Whoa! Wait a second, you mean to tell me that this is going to lead to people marrying an animal? It's already begun! Remember this lady she married her dog.

Narrator: *"We've all heard a dog's best friend. But for one woman, it's till death do us part for her and her pooch. Forty-seven-year-old Amanda Rogers was married 20 years ago but the marriage ended only after a few months. It seems like she was barking up the wrong tree with that guy. You might be wondering what kind of dog it was to win her over, have her walk down the aisle. Well, it was a terrier, its name is Sheba, it's also female, just like her. It's kind of like a lesbian romance. I hope they're not doing anything sexual. They did kiss during the ceremony. Of their new marriage, Amanda says, I couldn't think of anything I could need more from a life partner. Really though?"*

Yeah, really. this is what you get when you twist with God's design. A depraved mind! That's a sign that we're in the final stages and God is judging us. And you're doing things that ought not to be done. And it gets worse than that. In fact, here's some more depraved minds in action! We now have people in the media saying that zoosexuality, bestiality, is perfectly fine.

Jacob Appel: *"I would argue that all of them should be legal. Overarchingly for the same reason that the state really has very little interest controlling what people do in their own private lives in their own bedrooms unless it directly and negatively affects other people in a tangible way. I'm not convinced that any of those particular items, whether its bestiality, polygamy, incest, do have that effect on consenting adults or between human being and animals where consent really is not a meaningful question."*

Why should prostitution, polygamy, incest, and bestiality be legalized?

bigthink.com/jacobappel

Web Question Reports: *"Peter Singer, in your 2001 article Heavy Petting, you state that mutually satisfying sexual activities between humans can develop. Please explain."*

Peter Singer: *"I wondered if that one would come up. So, firstly, it was a book review, it wasn't really an article. I was reviewing a book that discussed this issue. I mean, it is a fact that there is sexual contact between some humans and animals, and I was raising the question why we have such a taboo on this."*

Because God said not to! And they used to get the death penalty! That's how serious it is. This is just flat out sick and it's no game! This kind of stuff really is coming like God warned about! And this is what's going on while most churches today are either complicit with it, which is half the church, the professing church, or if you know better, you are off in la-la land, or you do know better, and you've never once addressed this from the pulpit. Can I tell you something? Shame on you, and I'm talking to the ones that are born again Christians, including pastors and Sunday school teachers. And the people in pews, can't they speak up and say, pastor can we get the rest of the Scripture once in a while? Hey pastor, can you address this? Pastor, do you see what's going on in the news right now? They're appointing somebody who refuses to give a definition of a woman. Can we hear about this? Does the Bible talk about this?

Yeah, it does! But can we talk about it as a church? Can we get equipped? How do we respond, because we're supposed to be the salt and light. We are supposed to be the restrainers, specifically as we await the rapture. That's what the Scripture says. But how am I supposed to restrain if I don't know how to respond. And that's your job. Where are you? Not just behind the pulpit but where are the Christians demanding that from the churches and if you're not getting it from the church and they refuse to do it, then why are you supporting them? You better get out of there. Because you choose convenience instead of Biblical truth. That's why they continue.

"Former House Majority Leader Tom DeLay says not only is all hell breaking loose after the Supreme Court's ruling on gay marriage, but we're on the fast track to legalizing all new kinds of perversions including pedophilia and bestiality.

He also pointed to a "secret memo" from the Department of Justice when asked if the tax-exempt status of religious institutions could be pulled if they teach against gay marriage.

"We've already found a secret memo coming out of the Justice Department saying that they're now going after 12 new perversions, things like bestiality, polygamy, having sex with little boys and making that legal.

Not only that, but they have a whole list of strategies to go after the churches, the pastors, and any businesses that tries to assert their religious liberty. This is coming and it's coming like a tidal wave."

Why? Because even the church is going along with this because we've been taken over by enemies …fakers! To the point where now half the Church thinks homosexuality is okay. They talk about building your self-esteem. They are getting so in your face from rebelliousness in our country, that they've not only taken the rainbow and twisted it and celebrating sin, when it was a promise that God's not going to judge the world because of sin with a flood, but He's going to do it with fire. Now they have twisted the meaning of it, and that becomes their new symbol to celebrate sin. They are flaunting it in God's face! They launched it into space.

"On August 17th, 2016, Planting Peace launched the first pride flag into space, and declared space LGBTQ friendly. We quickly realized we didn't have the budget for this guy. So, we went with this guy, and used a high-altitude balloon.

Declaring space as LGBTQ friendly reinforces our universal message to our LGBTQ family."

Bad enough that they did that to the White House, basically in your face God! Dare I say, in your face God, to the country that was built on Christian principals! In your face God, right at the White House! But now you're saying, in your face God, we're going to orbit the planet to make sure you see this. What did our text open up with?

Romans 1:18: "The wrath of God is being revealed from Heaven against all the godlessness and wickedness of men who suppress the truth by their wickedness."

You have the audacity to flaunt your sin in the face of God in Heaven. So, what you are doing is exactly what He says is going to happen. You're storing up His wrath that is going to be poured out on you.

Romans 2:5: "But because of your stubbornness and your unrepentant heart, you are storing up wrath against yourself for the day of God's wrath, when His righteous judgment will be revealed."

He's going to have the last word on this. And for those who attend these churches that support this or for those who attend churches that refuse to teach on this, then you need to make up your mind with this meme we saw before.

Make up your minds, stop being two souls, double minded. Are you going to follow God or not? Are you going to support Biblical truth or not? Is it a Biblical marriage or not? Is it a Biblical relationship or not? Is it Biblical love or not? Which one is it, make up your mind! It can't be both.

WE CAN'T BE THE "BRIDE OF CHRIST" AND THE "GIRLFRIEND OF SATAN".

Now, because half of the so-called professing church is going along with this twisted relationship, twisted love, being produced by these fakers, enemies in the church, and the other half is off in la-la land with these fluffy teachings, false teachings, anything else but this, or you're just keeping your mouth shut on it. Out of fear or whatever it is called. Now we are the new haters. The Bible has now become the hate book and if you support what this hate book says, any of the verses we have been going over, any one of these things, you, not just pastors and churches, you are going to be hauled in for a meeting. Anyone who objects to this behavior is going to become a hater and you will have to be taken away because you no longer fit in their sinful system.

Interrogator: *"Thank you for coming down Mr. Wilson, I know you're a busy man, so we'll try and keep this short. Come on in and have a seat. So, for the record, your name is John Francis Wilson, and you live at 15 Clear Heights Drive. Could you clearly reply yes or no to my questions."*

John Wilson: *"Yes, I am John Wilson. Is this being recorded?"*

Interrogator: *"Are you a member of the Church of God on Springer Avenue?"*

John Wilson: *"Yes."*

Interrogator: *"Have you taken part in their pro-life meetings and marches?"*

John Wilson: *"Well, yes, but what does this have to do...?"*

Interrogator: *"And do you plan on attending this evening's meetings with this group?"*

John Wilson: *"Yes."*

Interrogator: *"Mr. Wilson are you aware that it is legal in this country to have an abortion?"*

John Wilson: *"Yes, but it hasn't always been that way."*

Interrogator: *"Are you aware that some health care providers have been attacked and murdered by members of groups like yours?"*

John Wilson: *"Hold on. We have nothing to do with those groups. We are peaceful people that are..."*

Interrogator: *"Are you aware that some health care providers have been attacked, Mr. Wilson?"*

John Wilson: *"We believe in preserving life and not taking it."*

Interrogator: *"Are you aware, Mr. Wilson, yes, or no? You are a member of three different right to life groups, you are a member of a number of evangelical Christian organizations. You've donated money to Christian Science Research and the Salvation Army, and you receive daily emails from radical organizations that encourage prayer for our government on matters of policy. You signed a number of petitions supporting the traditional definition of marriage and you frequently visit websites that are pro-Israel and others that believe in an imminent cataclysmic event. Your wife and children are also enrolled in or talking to many other radical anti-social organizations and people. Mr. Wilson, there is a lot more here. Are these the actions of a peaceful man and his family?"*

Now, for those of you thinking that this could never happen here in America, I'm telling you, it's right around the corner. Why? Because we, the Church in America, have been asleep at the wheel for so stinking long, and because we have become so complacent and in love with the things of the world instead of God, Who made this world. And because we continue to beat each other up and defeat the purpose of God, we are now paying a horrible price. The noose has slowly been put around our necks, while we're literally being entertained to death. And now, a global hatred of Christianity, is just around the corner because of homosexuality, solidified by the Supreme Court's Decision. Don't believe me? It's already happening!

"Why do we want equality, when do we want it, now! Why do we want equality!!"

Faith2Action Reports: *"We've been hearing about it for months but the battle for marriage isn't about equality. By trampling on marriage, homosexual activists want to reshape the culture into something that we won't even recognize. But this battle isn't about marriage, it's about driving the homosexual flag in yet another segment of society and using it as a club to silence all dissent to label anyone who disagrees as a hater. Just like someone visited the family research council after the Southern Poverty Law Center slapped them with a hate group label."*

Peter Sprigg, Family Research Council: *"In his backpack the police found 50 rounds of ammunition and 15 chick-fil-a sandwiches."*

Fox News Reports: *"Floyd Corkins had admitted that he intended to shoot and kill as many as possible of the staff of Family Research Council as he could. And he intended to smear the chick-fil-a sandwiches in the faces of his victims."*

Peter Sprigg: *"Corkins had chosen his target or multiple targets by looking at the website of the Southern Poverty Law Center. Because they had designated Family Research Council as a quote-unquote 'anti-gay hate group' and placed us on their hate map which is still on their website. That was how he chose us as a target."*

Faith2Action Reports: *"Once marriage is redefined, that becomes a foundation for Christian and traditional beliefs to be marginalized. It's no longer speculation. When Massachusetts courts redefined marriage, K-12 homosexual indoctrination intensified, and parental rights became a thing of the past.*

David Parker, parent: *"After the diversity book, we realized that the intention of the administrators and teachers was to affirm the relationships and gay marriage in the minds of children. When we went into the school, what we requested is parental notification when these issues are brought up by adults within the school and the option to opt our child out of this type of indoctrination."*

Tonia Parker, mother: *"You wish to affirm homosexuality to our son. You're presenting that which is sin as though it is not, to our son, and we cannot allow that."*

David Parker, parent: *"To make a long story short, the accommodation they gave was to put me in handcuffs and send me to jail."*

Faith2Action Reports: *"This battle isn't about marriage. It's about freedom."*

David Parker: *"They were willing to handcuff a father and send him to jail. It was a 6X8 cell, filthy, but I felt that I didn't have a choice at that point, in order to fulfill my role and duty as a father."*

Defend Marriage, Defend Freedom: *"If we care about our freedom, we had better use it now. Help us warn the church!*

And you wonder why I'm preaching on this now! Folks, we better speak up, this is really happening, the persecution has already begun. And it's about to get even worse! And notice it wasn't just a Pastor. But a Christian Father, who simply objected to his son being taught homosexuality in school, was labeled as a hate crime, and was handcuffed and thrown into prison…in America! Not just a pastor, but now even your average born-again Christian!

Chapter Seven

God's Judgment with a Depraved Mind

In the previous chapters, we've seen the perversions of the world and the church. Their twisting of God's truth and His Biblical love. They say it's eros instead of agapao. That is their reasoning as to why we should allow any and all sinful behavior. But as we look at what Biblical love is, we saw that God reveals He is love by giving us mercy, compassion, kindness, graciousness, patience, faithfulness and goodness. I'll take that love over the sick, twisted, perverted one of today. And that leads us to the next twisting, which they are using to justify present conditions, and that is, they are twisting Biblical relationships.

They twisted the rainbow and now have twisted the Biblical view of relationships i.e., marriage between a man and a woman. Now that has opened Pandora's box. This twisting has led not only to homosexuality and lesbianism but now to polygamy, gender fluidity, pedophilia, and bestiality. Why? Because as God warned when you go down this route, He will hand you over to a depraved mind and you will start doing things that ought not to be done! I didn't say that God did.

Romans 1:28-32: "Furthermore, since they did not think it worthwhile to retain the knowledge of God, he gave them over to a depraved mind, to do what ought not to be done. They have become filled with every kind of wickedness, evil, greed and depravity. They are full of envy, murder, strife, deceit and malice. They are gossips, slanderers, God-haters, insolent, arrogant and boastful; they invent ways of doing evil; they disobey their parents, they are senseless, faithless, heartless, ruthless. Although they know God's righteous decree that those who do such things deserve death, they not only continue to do these very things but also approve of those who practice them."

The Supreme Court is one aspect, but dare I say not just the Supreme Court approving those who practice that, as you're seeing, the many enemies within the church is approving that as well. As we saw before, the stat now for those who profess to be Christians in the American church today is now 50 percent who have no problem with homosexuality. What Bible are you reading? Apparently, you're not. But that's what's going on.

The Greek word there for depraved is "adokimos" which is "a" or "negative, no or not" and "dokimos" "accepted, approved, pleasing." So "a" "dokimos" means, "no or not accepted, no or not approved, no or not pleasing." This is why, because of their rebellion, their minds are given over to doing things that are not acceptable, not to be approved and not pleasing at all! And I want to show you what that depraved mind looks like.

Here is a man interviewing a lady about "What is a woman?" And you tell me if she doesn't have a depraved mind. I say that deliberately because again it's not that, that's just weird, that's insane, because we come up with all these adjectives. But I'm encouraging you to get into the Biblical adjective. What you are about to see is a depraved mind in action and it's a conversation that a man is having with somebody who is a part of the crowd that is dictating what's going on in our school system and things of that nature. The conversation simply put is, "What is a Woman?" Which we have heard about in the news. It isn't just wrong. We laughed about it. We're going, that's crazy, no, you are going to see a depraved mind in action over something as simplistic as what is a woman. Look at this.

Matt Walsh: *"Veering significantly over to the disturbing end of the spectrum is my interview with Dr. Michelle Forcier who is as you'll hear her proudly identify herself, a gender affirming pediatrician, also an abortionist. We flew up to Providence, Rhode Island to speak to Dr. Forcier. She was friendly enough at first, and what we found in many of the interviews that you'll see in "What is a Woman?" is that gender ideologues are very polite and nice right up until the moment when you express any skepticism at all. But before we get to that point where things really start to sort of fall apart, let's get to know Michelle a little."*

Dr. Michelle Forcier: *"My name is Michelle Forcier and I have a medical degree from the University of Connecticut residency, University of Utah, pediatrics and I've worked for a number of different Planned Parenthoods for 20 years. I do advanced contraception and abortion as well as gender hormones and sort of looking at the whole sort of schema of gender sex and reproductive justice."*

Matt Walsh: *"So, you've done a lot of work in this field, can you just start by telling us at what age can a child begin to transition into another gender or identify themselves as a gender different from how they were born?"*

Dr. Michelle Forcier: *"Well, I mean there's research and data that show that babies and infants understand differences in gender. Some children figure out their gender really early and the reason why we say that's interesting or important is because they're figuring out their gender identity is not necessarily congruent with their sex assigned at birth."*

Matt Walsh: *"When the doctor sees the penis and says this is a male, has a sex of male, that's an arbitrary distinction."*

Dr. Michelle Forcier: *"Telling that family, based on that little penis that your child is absolutely 100 percent male identified no matter what else occurs in their life. That's not correct."*

Matt Walsh: *"So, what does gender affirmation care? You're a big proponent of, if we walk through, a child is sitting down with you, is questioning their gender, what's the gender affirmation process?"*

Dr. Michelle Forcier: *"Affirmation means that as a pediatrician, as someone who says my job is to provide the best medical care for you, is I need to listen really carefully and how I put it in words for kids so that they can understand it, is tell me your story. Where have you been in terms of your gender and your gender identity? Where are you right now? And more excitingly, where would you like to be in the future?"*

Matt Walsh: *"Have you ever met a four-year-old who believes in Santa Claus?"*

Dr. Michelle Forcier: *"Yes."*

Matt Walsh: *"So, this is someone who believes that a fat man is traveling through the sky and a flying reindeer at lightning speed, coming down his chimney with presents?"*

Dr. Michelle Forcier: *"Yes."*

Matt Walsh: *"Would you say this is someone who maybe has a tenuous grasp on reality?"*

Dr. Michelle Forcier: *"They have an appropriate four-year-old handle on the reality that's very real for them."*

Matt Walsh: *"Agreed, agreed, but Santa Claus is real for them, but Santa Claus is not actually real."*

Dr. Michelle Forcier: *"Yeah, but Santa Claus does deliver their Christmas presents."*

Matt Walsh: *"But he's not real though."*

Dr. Michelle Forcier: *"To that child they are."*

Matt Walsh: *"When I see a child who believes in Santa Claus and then, let's say this is a boy and he says I'm a girl, this is someone who can't distinguish between fantasy and reality so how could you take that as a reality?"*

Dr. Michelle Forcier: *"I would say, as a pediatrician and as a parent, I would say how wonderful my four-year-old and their imagination is."*

In the studio:

Matt Walsh: *"Now one of the hardest things, as we did this film, especially interviewing somebody like that, is not like my instinct just to yell at them to begin with, but it's kind of a short film if it's just me going around yelling at people. The objective here is to ask questions and that's all we did. The whole film is just, ask questions. And let gender ideology essentially hang itself, is the idea. And to show is this something that can withstand scrutiny or not. Even just basic scrutiny, and what we discovered is that it can't. So, what's happening in that exchange is, first of all she says, talking about a child who sits down with her is, she wants to know about their gender journey and where would you like to be in the future. So, she's talking about a child's five-year gender plan.*

The point I was trying to get across to her is that children don't have a grasp on reality. Even if in theory people could choose their own gender which they can't, but if they could, it wouldn't make sense to say that a child could choose it. Children believe in Santa Claus so what do they know about reality? If a child is four years old and believes that not only Santa Claus is real, but that fairies and dragons live appropriately in this kind of fantasy world. The boy says I'm a girl, that claim exists within the same fantasy world. This is just imagination. This is a kid that just doesn't understand the distinction between fantasy and reality. So, how do they make these determinations? But then again, as we found there, Michelle wouldn't even affirm that Santa doesn't exist. I was unclear about that also. Do you actually think that Santa exists? What's happening? But as you are talking to these people you feel yourself going slightly insane. So, it was a pretty bewildering exchange there, but it only gets weirder from here. Let's keep watching."

Back to the interview:

Matt Walsh: *"Male sperm, that's what makes me male?"*

Dr. Michelle Forcier: *"No, your sperm don't make you male."*

Matt Walsh: *"Then what does?"*

Dr. Michelle Forcier: *"It's a constellation."*

Matt Walsh: *"In reality, in truth, okay?"*

Dr. Michelle Forcier: *"Who's truth are we talking about?"*

Matt Walsh: *"The same truth that says we are sitting in this room. Right now, you and I."*

Dr. Michelle Forcier: *"No, you're not listening."*

Matt Walsh: *"If I see a chicken laying eggs and I say that's a female chicken laying eggs, did I assign female or am I just observing a physical reality that's happening in the world?"*

Dr. Michelle Forcier: *"Does a chicken have gender identity? Does a chicken cry? Does a chicken commit suicide? Let's refrain because you're trying ..."*

Matt Walsh: *"A chicken has sex like any biological organism."*

Dr. Michelle Forcier: *"An assigned gender, but a chicken doesn't have a gender identity."*

Matt Walsh: *"So we assign female to chickens when they lay eggs?"*

Dr. Michelle Forcier: *"We assume they're female if they lay eggs."*

Back in the studio:

Matt Walsh: *"That right there will go down for me as one of the most, probably and every other thing that makes it on this particular list in the film, but certainly one of the most outrageous exchanges I've ever had with anybody, and of course, see, this is what happens when you start asking questions to the proponent of gender ideology. They end up backing themselves into various corners and have to make increasingly wilder sort of claims to get themselves out of the corners that they've backed themselves into.*

So, when you are talking about sex for example, like it's all on a spectrum and sex is something that is, as she says in our conversation, she says that sex is assigned at birth. Like doctors are just deciding this arbitrarily. Well, if that's the nature of sex, then what about other organisms aside from human beings? We could also say that when a chicken is laying eggs, oh, that's a female chicken. Are we assigning that? Is that just something we decided? That the chicken is female? Or is the chicken female? If the chicken is female, then that would tell us something about the nature of biological sex, which is that it's not assigned, it's observed.

But she can't go along with that and so she starts talking about the chicken's gender identity and whether chickens commit suicide. And it doesn't get much better from there."

Back to the interview:

Matt Walsh: *"At what age does the medical transition begin with medication?"*

Dr. Michelle Forcier: *"So medical affirmation usually begins when the patient says they're ready for it. So that could be a kiddo who is just starting puberty and panicking because they're getting breast buds or their penis is getting bigger and busier and they're worried about all kinds of masculine changes and that way puberty blockers, which are completely reversible and don't have permanent effects are wonderful, because we can put that pause on puberty, just like you were listening to music. You put the pause on, and we stopped the blockers and puberty would go right back to where it was, to the next note in the song, just delayed for that period of time."*

In the studio:

Matt Walsh: *"So, this is a part, from later in the film, as we start to get into more of the specifics about puberty blockers. And I'm not going to say myself right now, a lot in response to that, because you have to go watch the film. Because as I said I'm asking questions and we don't just ask questions of people on this side. We bring in other people. So, there's a little bit of a back and forth here, but we're going to get a response in the film to this claim that puberty can 'just pause it' as she said, like music. Does the human body work that way? I mean, is that the way it works? Where you can take a drug to intentionally interfere with certain normal healthy processes, and you could take them and there's no negative consequences? At all? Just stop taking the drug and pick up where you left off?*

Which of course, the interesting thing is that even if that was true, which it isn't, as you'll see in the film. But even if it was true, then wouldn't that mean, if a child is taking puberty blockers to stop their normal development and then we're just putting it on pause for, let's say, for five years, and then they decide, okay I don't want to take this anymore. Well, at a minimum they're going to be five years behind in their growth and development. So, even according to her version of events, at a minimum you're going to have stunted growth, and you are going to have someone who is behind in their physical development. Actually, the consequences are a lot worse than that. As we discover in the film and as we get into in this next exchange about the puberty blockers themselves. What are they? What do they do? What is their actual purpose?"

Back to the interview:

Matt Walsh: *"One of the drugs used is Lupron, right? Which has been used to chemically castrate sex offenders?"*

Dr. Michelle Forcier: *"You know what, I'm not sure if we should continue with this interview because it seems like it's going in a particular direction."*

Matt Walsh: *"Well, you're a medical professional?"*

Dr. Michelle Forcier: *"I am a medical professional."*

Matt Walsh: *"You don't want to talk about the drugs that you give to kids?"*

Dr. Michelle Forcier: *"Again, I am a physician and I use medication. You're choosing exploitative words, drugs I give..."*

Matt Walsh: *"I'm choosing a chemical word that was in a dictionary."*

Dr. Michelle Forcier: *"That's not a correct term for puberty blocking."*

Matt Walsh: *"I could look it up on my phone. I'm pretty sure if I looked it up..."*

Dr. Michelle Forcier: *"You can look it up on your phone."*

Matt Walsh: *"Dictionary: 'Chemical Castration, noun. The medical definition to bring about a marked reduction in the production of androgens and especially testosterones."*

Dr. Michelle Forcier: *"And I'm saying as a pediatrician who takes care of hundreds of these kids, when you use that terminology, you are being malignant and harmful."*

Matt Walsh: *"You mean there are some who would say that giving chemical castration drugs to kids is malignant and harmful."*

Dr. Michelle Forcier: *"It's about the context of caring for a child and seeing the suffering that kids can have that have not been in affirmative home situations."*

Back in the studio:

Matt Walsh: *"Well that was the part in our conversation where things got a bit contentious, but I wouldn't say that's when they started to get contentious. Actually, what we discovered in doing these interviews is that I kind of knew going in, I had certain points in mind where, okay, when I ask this question, things might get a little bit tense, and I know that's more of a challenging question. What I found so often in these interviews is that things got tense much earlier than I originally thought they would. There were questions that I thought would be really easy for the person I'm talking to, that turned out to be not easy at all. Questions like what's the difference between sex and gender? That's supposed to be a softball. But even with that, things start to go off the rails in a lot of these interviews. When I asked a question like, what we found is that these people, these gender ideologues, especially the ones that are in this industry, and are making a lot of money off of promoting gender confusion, especially in kids, it's that what we found is that they are not prepared to encounter any skepticism, at all. They are not prepared to answer any questions. The only questions they are prepared to answer are the questions that are not really questions at all. Questions like, 'How meaningful is it to you to be* *able to help people in their gender journey?' Like those kinds of questions or it's just a set up for them to give a pre-planned, canned speech.*

So, by the time we got to this exchange it'd already gotten pretty tense. I asked her about Lupron. Now this is a drug that she gives to kids and as we hear from somebody else in the film, Scott Nugent, who has experience with these kinds of drugs, personal experience. This drug, in particular, is a drug, actually by definition, chemical castration, which is why I wasn't planning on doing this. But when I pulled out my phone to look up the definition of chemical castration, she said chemical castration is an exploitative word and I'm being malignant and harmful by using that word. Well, look up the definition of chemical castration and that is a puberty blocker. That is, by definition, when you give a kid a puberty blocker you are performing chemical castration on the kid, period!

We know this because Lupron, specifically, has been used to chemically castrate sex offenders. Did you notice in that exchange, by the way, she didn't deny? She takes issue with the word that I'm using. She threatens to get up and storm out. She's offended by the way that I'm phrasing it, the words. But she never says, oh no, that's totally incorrect. Lupron does not do that; Lupron has never been used that way. She doesn't say that because she can't.

And finally, we get to THE question, which is the question I ask everyone, which is 'What is a Woman?' And it's probably not going to surprise you by now that she doesn't exactly have an answer for it. Let's listen to what she comes up with."

Back to the interview:

Matt Walsh: *"So, we're going on this journey, boys can be girls, girls can be boys, men can be women, women can be men. It makes me wonder, what is a woman?"*

Dr. Michelle Forcier: *"What is a woman? A woman is someone who claims that as their identity. It could be many things to many people."*

In the studio:

Matt Walsh: *That was her answer. Well, a woman is anyone. And that was by the way not to give any spoilers away, but that is the answer, from the left to the question, which is the same thing as a non-answer. But that is the answer, the woman is someone who says that's her identity. And of course, everyone who gives me that answer in the film, I have a follow-up. A woman is someone who identifies as a woman. What are they identifying as, and around and around we go. Because they don't have an answer to the question. This is a medical doctor who can't tell you what a woman is. I mean this is someone who if someone goes to her as a man and says, 'I'm really a woman, I want to transition into a woman,' she will help facilitate that process and yet she doesn't know what the word means.*

She doesn't actually know, by her own testimony, when someone says, 'I want to transition to a woman,' she doesn't even know what that means. What are you transitioning into? She has no idea. As we found over and over again in the film. That was just a few minutes of the film. Only one person of the dozens that we spoke to, and I can tell you right now that what we heard in those clips, I don't think any of it qualifies as quite the craziest thing we heard. The chicken part gets pretty close, still not all the way there. There's so much more that you need to see, but you have to go to 'whatisawoman.com?' and subscribe to see a lot more of where that came from. I promise you."

I left that there on purpose so you can go do more research. Believe it or not, that's just the tip of the tip of the iceberg, of that kind of mentality. How do you wrap your brain around that? I mean how do you describe what you just read? How do you describe what was coming out of that lady's mouth, her brain, etc.? The Bible calls it, that's depraved! That's not just wrong, it's "adokimos," it's not to be accepted and it's not pleasing. We should never approve that! The problem is that because the church is either compromised on this issue or a bunch of chicken livers and choose to keep their mouths shut on the issue. I get it, the world doesn't know any better. They don't know Christ. I'm not condoning it, but I get it, because they don't know Christ, but the Church?! What's happened is these people are infiltrating all sectors of society with that lady's mindset. She's not an anomaly.

These people in that camp, this is literally their mindset. I believe it's a depraved mind and I think it's an act of judgment from God. Just like He said, you keep denying me and you keep turning from me, even though I'll give you tons of evidence, you have the audacity to do that. Even though you started out as a Christian nation, I'm going to hand you over and you keep it up, you're going to make that final stage and you're going to do "adokimos." This stuff is going to be literally unbelievable and that's where we're at. These people are in the government, the medical community, the school community. This article just happened this week.

Child abuse is what I call it, at least it used to be called that. But New York city schools are spending over $200 thousand dollars on drag queen shows for children. I said it before, and I'll say it again, get your kids out of the sewer pipe. Homeschool, get them out now! How bad does it have to get from these depraved minds, who are in charge of the school system, the government, the medical community, Hollywood, cartoons, you name it. There's supposed to be this baby formula shortage going on and you're spending $200 thousand dollars on drag queens reading to kids. Who does that? It's somebody who has a depraved mind! Because we have kept our mouths shut for so long, they have now infiltrated all sectors of the church that really control the shape and direction of the church, the same way as these guys. These depraved minds have been allowed to go on for so long that they are in all sectors of society.

Now I mentioned Hollywood and cartoons. I remember growing up in the 80s, the worst cartoon we had was Wile E. Coyote getting squished by a rock or Bugs Bunny got hit over the head with a hammer. But I remember, even in the 80s, it started to turn, and cartoons were no longer cartoons. It was Captain Planet; it was the environmental movement. Save the planet, and then they started weaving in the four elements which is basically, witchcraft, paganism, and things of that nature. That was in my generation. Well, now that's child's play. These people with their depraved minds are twisting kid's minds, getting them to go along with this depravity, in cartoons. I'm going to share with you a recent cartoon and you guess which network this aired on. The cartoon starts with a lady singing a song, dressed in bright colors and makeup and a crown on her head. In the background on what looks like a float are three dinosaurs holding up rainbow flags. The dinosaurs look like two females with a little one, a child, standing in the middle of the two. The words of the song are as follows:

"This family is marching one by one, Hurrah! Hurrah! This family is marching one by one, Hurrah! Hurrah! This family has two mommies, they love each other so proudly, and they all go marching in the big parade! Families marching two by two, Hurrah! Hurrah! Families marching two by two, Hurrah! Hurrah! This family has two daddies, they love each other so proudly and they all go marching in the big parade. Come on friends! Families marching three by three, Hurrah! Hurrah! Families marching three by three, Hurrah! Hurrah! These Babas are non-binary, they love each other so proudly, and they all go marching in the big parade, Hurrah! Hurrah!"

That was Blue's Clues, the new and approved Blue's Clues. How many parents right now have a clue? Oh, you're watching Blue's Clues, that's a good show. Maybe it used to be. Maybe, and this stuff is on there. A non-binary dolphin? Who thinks of that? Who puts that in a kid's cartoon? If we only had some sort of label to describe that. A depraved mind! That is not acceptable. That should not be accepted, it's bad enough you're doing this to adults, but you do it to kids. You can call it WOKE, call it POLITICALLY CORRECT, call it whatever. It's DEPRAVED!

And frankly, even though this next one is a parody this is what these depraved minds want us to accept. This video opens with a Ken doll laying back in a chair at a beauty salon. The announcer comes on saying,

"New from Mattel, Barbie's boyfriend is getting a much needed and way more inclusive makeover, introducing 'Pregnant Ken.' He's a man with a baby. His belly lets you know that he's pregnant and his beard lets you know he's a man. Because men can get pregnant just like women, in fact there's no definition of women. We literally have no idea what a woman is. Pregnant Ken does all the normal things every birthing person does, like chest feed, then hides his breasts with chest binders.

He rocks the baby to sleep with his supple masculine arms and Ken being a man and therefore a good driver, can even put the baby in the back of the car for a fun drive around town. But not everyone in Barbie World is as open-minded as Ken. Another doll says, 'Men can't get pregnant, hey, wait a minute, you're just a woman with hormones.' But Ken yells at her, 'Shut up bigot!' And he slaps her across the face. Tell your birthing people to buy you a pregnant Ken today because why should women be the only ones who can experience the miracle of getting an abortion? 'My body my choice.' Available in the non-gender specific toy aisle at Target, adjacent to the chestnuts for kids. Not legal for sale in Florida, Texas, or Saudi Arabia."

That would be funny if that wasn't really what they want us to accept! Good thing these depraved mind cartoons and schools and individuals have no effect on kid's minds. Between Hollywood, cartoons, and schools, what I am about to show you, not too long-ago people would have been thrown in jail for. This is the effect of what Hollywood, the school system, and individuals, have done to the kids. They've twisted kid's minds that are becoming depraved as well. And when they begin to display that depraved behavior, the depraved adults celebrate it. Here is one example:

Matt Walsh: *"Now what you are about to see happened on live TV, on a major network, in front of a live studio audience. I didn't dig this up from the darkest fringes of the internet, this is as mainstream as it gets. It's what Disney promotes and supports. So, here's the time when Good Morning America featured an 11-year-old boy in drag. The child's stage name is Desmond is Amazing. Everyone in the building, including the hosts, including Michael Strahan as one of the hosts, seem to very much agree that what you are about to see is indeed amazing."*

Michael Strahan: *"Please welcome Desmond is Amazing.*
The audience cheers and claps as Desmond parades down the aisle to get to where the hosts of the show are sitting. He then takes a seat next to them to start the interview.

Michael Strahan: *"Hello, Desmond, how are you?"*

Co-host: *"Thank you for being here! I love that you love root beer, caffeine free. I can get on board with that."*

Desmond: *"My mom doesn't like me drinking caffeine."*

Co-host: *"Does it make you hyper?"*

Desmond nods his head signifying a yes.

Co-host: *"Yeah, me too. They don't like it when I drink caffeine either, but Desmond you're one of the youngest and first, drag queen, slash kids."*

The audience yells, cheers and claps at that comment.

Co-host: *"I heard that you've gotten messages from young adults that look up to you for you being who you are. What are some of the notes you've gotten?"*

Desmond: *"Some of the notes I've gotten are like, you inspire me very much and I wish I could have had the support that you have when I was a child."*

Back in the studio

Matt Walsh: *"Now if you are listening to the video podcast you have been spared the worst of what we just experienced altogether. Although you can't fully appreciate just how dark and deranged it was because Desmond, the 11-year-old drag kid, quote-unquote, prances out on stage in women's clothes, makeup caked on his face, dances for the adoring crowd of grown adults, at one-point lays himself out prostrate on the stage, while creepy Michael Strahan stares and claps, and then he sits down for a lengthy interview. Later in this segment that was aired on Disney's ABC, even though Disney totally is not trying to groom children at all, later in the segment, three adult drag queens are brought out on stage with Desmond, in their full cross-dressing costumes, woman face fully on, and they proceed to give Desmond gifts of make-up and quote-unquote dance classes. Take a look at this:*

Back at Disney's ABC the three adult drag queens are now sitting next to Desmond. In front of them is a table of all the gifts that they have brought him.

Co-Host: *"You guys want to tell us what's out here."*

Drag Queen #1: *"Well, I drew Desmond a picture of a little green-haired lady. It's to bring you good luck and prosperity in your future."*

Desmond: *"I eat iceberg lettuce."*

Drag Queen #1: *"It's good to eat iceberg lettuce for roughage, ok, there you go."*

Desmond: *"With tomatoes and cucumbers."*

Drag Queen #1: *"Absolutely!"*

Drag Queen #2: *"And I brought you a gift basket of some of my favorites. Let me hand it to you, because I think you need to have it in your hands. It is some of my favorite makeup essentials that I use."*

Once again, the audience cheers and claps.

Back in the studio

Matt Walsh: *"I will never understand so many things we are seeing here, but one of them is how every woman is not insulted when they see drag queens. I know so many are, in fact, but every woman should be insulted because leaving aside the worst part about this, which is the fact there's a kid there, we'll get back to that in a second. But you see that, and that is what they think of you. That's their impression of you. It is no different from blackface, it is female blackface. It is mockery of womanhood. This is what they think you are. This is their female impression. And if it seems cartoonish and degrading that's because it is. And that's how they see femininity, as a degraded cartoonish thing.*

By the way if you are wondering where the father is in all of this surprisingly or maybe not surprisingly, he is in the picture. He's literally in the picture. He's in the audience during this segment. He's one of the greasy disgusting guys, staring and clapping while the young boy is paraded around in cross-dressing burlesque gear. Desmond may as well be wearing a sandwich board sign which announces, 'I am a sexual abuse victim' because his abuse is on full display for all to see and the audience loves every minute of it, and ABC loves it, and Disney loves it."

How do you describe that? **Romans 1**, it's a society in the last stages of destruction with a depraved mind! And not long ago if somebody actually did that to a child you'd go to jail. It's child abuse, depraved and ought not to be done! But how quickly it has been twisted to be acceptable behavior, paraded in our face, repeatedly, overtly, and what is this month? It's a whole month dedicated to this kind of depravity.

Now if you don't think this is a spiritual war on our country, that was founded on Biblical principles and on God's word and the church, let's remind ourselves of the motive and intent of these people that's recorded in Congressional records back in 1987 called The Homosexual Manifesto. We were warned that this was a spiritual war coming, specifically on Christianity and the irony is that these people say that when we disagree with them and we promote Biblical values, traditional marriage values, relationships, which was what our country was founded upon as well. We are the ones that are guilty of a 'hate crime.' We're haters.

What I am about to share with you, they told us on Congressional records what they were going to do back in 1987 and either we didn't take it serious or again this is the fruit of compromise. Dare I say again, being a chicken liver and not speaking up, this is a deliberate attack. What you're about to see, keep in mind, their definition of a hate crime. If ever there was a hate crime in action and this is in Congressional records, it's this:

"This is the Gay Manifesto, by Michael Swift, first published in Gay Community News February 15ᵗʰ through the 21ˢᵗ in 1987. It is also

reprinted in the Congressional Record. This is what it states: 'We shall sodomize your sons, emblems of your feeble masculinity, of your shallow dreams and vulgar lies.

We shall seduce them in your schools, in your dormitories, in your gymnasiums, in your locker rooms, in your sports arenas, in your seminaries, in your youth groups, in your movie theater bathrooms, in your army bunk houses, in your truck stops, in all your male clubs, in your house of Congress, whenever men are with men together. Your sons will become our minions and do our biddings. They will be recast into our image.

All laws banning homosexual activity will be revoked. Instead, legislation shall be passed which engenders love between men. All homosexuals stand together as brothers. We shall triumph only when we present a common face to the vicious heterosexual enemy. If you dare to cry faggot, fairy, queer, at us, we will stab you in your cowardly hearts and defile your dead, puny bodies.

We will unmask the powerful homosexuals who masquerade as heterosexuals. You will be shocked and frightened when you find that your presidents and their sons, your industrialist, your senators, your mayors, your generals, your athletes, your film stars, your television personalities, your civic leaders, your priests are not the safe, familiar heterosexual figures you assumed them to be.

We are everywhere; we have infiltrated your ranks. Be careful when you speak of homosexuals because we are always among you; we may be sitting across the desk from you; we may be sleeping in the same bed with you.

All churches who condemn us will be closed. Our only gods are handsome young men. For us too much is not enough. All males who insist on remaining stupidly heterosexual will be tried in homosexual courts of justice and will become invisible men.

*We shall rewrite history. History filled and debased with your
heterosexual lies and distortions. We shall be victorious because we are
filled with the ferocious bitterness of the oppressed who have been forced
to place seemingly bit parts in your dumb heterosexual shows throughout
the age. We too are capable of firing guns and manning the barricades of
the ultimate revolution.*

*Tremble, hetero swine, when we appear before you without our masks. '
Have you heard or read this article before? Why not?"*

Gee, who's guilty of a hate crime? Because of the church being
complacent, apathetic, compromised, and silent. Now what is their
definition of hate crimes? If there ever was a hate crime, that's a hate
crime. These depraved minds are now persecuting anyone who disagrees
with their depraved minds and now they are saying that anyone who
agrees with Biblical values is guilty of hate crimes.

I'm not advocating as a Christian any "hate" or "violence" or
"bodily harm" to you, but by your own words, that's exactly what your
agenda is to me and my family, my children and to my Church and to my
country! And we better speak up and speak out or these depraved minds
are not only going to continue to bring the wrath of God upon our country,
but it will be used to silence and get rid of us!

Now the key word for that is hypocrisy and what do we see in the
church? The Church is compromising which is digging our own grave.

CHURCH COMPROMISE

- Christian Book Publishers are now printing and supporting Pro-
lesbian, gay, bisexual, and transgender books.

- The United Church of Christ with its 5,100 Churches across America
is now supporting the 9th annual Gay Games in Ohio.

- The United Methodist Church is granting same-sex benefits to its employees involved in same-sex marriages.

- A Baptist Church in Kentucky is now holding gay weddings.

- Tony Campolo, a Christian leader/author has not only changed his stance on homosexuality, but he even recently stated, "A new day is dawning in Christianity" where he hopes all his "fellow Christians lovingly welcome all gay and lesbians in the Church. I have concluded that sexual orientation is almost never a choice and I have seen how damaging it can be to try to 'cure' someone from being gay."

- The Episcopal Church has now officially joined the Presbyterian Church and the United Church of Christ in becoming another mainline denomination to embrace gay marriage rites and has now officially 'axed' 'man and woman' from their institution of marriage clause in their canon.

- A Southern Baptist Pastor, Danny Cortez from Los Angeles, recently announced his change of mind on homosexuality and same-sex relationships. He acknowledged that his change of heart put him at odds with the SBC's confession of faith, but the Church voted on May 18 of this year not to dismiss him and instead to, 'Become a Third Way Church.'

- Soon after this he was invited to attend a 'gay pride' reception at the White House with the President. And later in a letter Cortez wrote, "This is a huge step for a Southern Baptist Church."

- And speaking of huge steps, for the first time in history, a national Christian denomination, the United Church of Christ, is suing the state of North Carolina to allow gay marriage.

- And another first is the Church of England. They are now considering a "Transgender Baptism Service" to "bless into God's family the new identities of Christians who have undergone gender transition."

- And recently, the Washington National Cathedral not only hosted its first transgender priest celebrating "LGBT month." But Gary Hall, the chief ecclesiastical leader and executive officer of the National Cathedral said that "Homophobia and Heterosexism is a sin."

God's standard has now become a sin in the church. That's how twisted it's become, not just in the world but in the church. And this just recently happened. Let me give you a couple headlines. A Chicago

preacher leads a sermon in drag. That's an Episcopal Church.

And then this was just two weeks ago. A Methodist church's first drag queen pastor, who says, "God is nothing," is a gender-bending minister for the nation's third largest denomination. He also says, "Queerness is divine." That was two weeks ago. Do you see a pattern here? You open the floodgates, you bought into this twisted love, we just gotta love these people. Yes, we love them, but we don't compromise the truth. But the church accepted that and thought it was going to stop there. Excuse me? Folks, do you have any idea what these people are doing? Talk about hypocrisy. They're

celebrating people going to hell! How can you celebrate that? That's one of the most unloving sinful rotten things you could ever do! You're supposed to be a Christian! Who in their right mind would do that? You're a follower of Jesus Christ! You're supposed to love like Jesus!

And He loved people enough to tell them the truth about the dangers that lie ahead with undealt sin, all sin, not just homosexuality. In fact, Jesus has choice words for people who act like that!

Matthew 5:29: "If your right eye causes you to sin, gouge it out and throw it away. It is better for you to lose one part of your body than for your whole body to be thrown into HELL."

Mark 9:43: "If your hand causes you to sin, cut it off. It is better for you to enter life maimed than with two hands to go into HELL, where the fire never goes out."

Mark 9:45: "And if your foot causes you to sin, cut it off. It is better for you to enter life crippled than to have two feet and be thrown into HELL."

Hey, you've got to take sin seriously because if sin isn't dealt with through the forgiveness of Jesus Christ on the cross preaching the truth of the gospel, which is what all of us need, no matter what sin you are involved in, you end up where? You end up in hell. And these people say we don't even talk about sin, and we actually affirm and accept sin and promote sin. Jesus said, you better cut it off. It gets worse.

Matthew 23:15: "Woe to you, teachers of the law and Pharisees, you hypocrites! You travel over land and sea to win a single convert, and when he becomes one, you make him twice as much a son of HELL as you are."

Could it be that these people that are doing this are like James is saying, they are fakers, enemies within the church? I know we Christians can make some big mistakes and we can act like non-Christians sometimes but how do you promote something like this? And say it's perfectly fine? Well, maybe that's the problem. You're in danger of hell, even though you are behind the pulpit or you're on a church board, whatever, promoting all of this because you don't know Christ either.

Matthew 23:33: "You snakes! You brood of vipers! How will you escape being condemned to Hell?"

These are some pretty strong words for hypocrites. And you see, that's the problem. Only God knows the heart, but maybe the reason why these people in the church are compromising doing this hypocritical behavior, is because they're fake, you're not headed to Heaven either. And the hypocrisy gets even worse.

Now, let's go back to the other camp. They are hypocrites because they say if we disagree, we are guilty of a hate crime. What's the other term that they use, "You need to be loving and tolerant." Tolerance is the new word, right? Alright, then why don't you tolerate my beliefs? That's called being a hypocrite. You sit there and say that I am guilty of a hate crime if I disagree with you, even though I don't hate you and I don't advocate any violence. But you say you hate me, and you do advocate violence.

But the point is this, how in the world could you ever call yourself a Christian, a follower of Jesus Christ, Who loved people so much that He died for all their sins to be forgiven and dealt with, so you could go to Heaven and not hell. Either you keep your mouth shut about this or compromise on it and actually celebrate it. It's because I love my neighbor that I have to take this stance against these depraved minds! Anything to the contrary is the most unloving hypocritical thing I could ever do as a Christian! If you don't think this is a deliberate attack on us, Christians and Christianity and our Christian heritage as a nation then let's look at some more hypocritical behavior.

But that's only half the problem. If the church is not only guilty of being hypocritical by compromising, but they're also being hypocritical with duplicit behavior like these people are. We've already seen how Christian businesses are being attacked and how Christian Churches are now being threatened with closure and Christian Pastors and Christians, being jailed for not supporting this decision, right? However, lest you think this is not a deliberate attack on Christianity alone, have you ever noticed that other religions are also against homosexuality? But you don't hear anything about that in the media! Check out what the Muslims are doing with their cakes! Do they get in trouble when they refuse to bake a gay cake?

Next News Network: *"The gay rights movement has reached a breaking point once again and it's on the national stage, but something is missing. Now if you have been following the outcry over the Religious Freedom Restoration Act, the gay rights movement is furious over the law that was passed in Indiana. They say it'll allow Christians to discriminate against them. Well, shortly after the bill was passed a reporter entered Memories Pizza in Walkerton, Indiana. They asked if they would cater a gay wedding and just like their bakery counterpart in Lakewood, Colorado, who refused to bake a cake for a gay wedding, the O'Connor family refused the hypothetical question of catering a gay wedding. Now with all the controversy over the issue I thought to myself, did anyone go to a Jewish or a Muslim bakery or pizza joint and ask them? Well, ask and you shall receive.*

At a Muslim Bakery

Steven Crowder: *"What's really important is getting the picture and the writing just right, so it's going to be me and Benny, and I want it to say Ben and Steven forever on the top and then on the bottom it'll say, same-sex, legal now, congratulations."*
But she shakes her head no! And he goes to a Jewish bakery.

Steven Crowder: *"But everyone keeps sending me somewhere else. They said this is what you do here."*

Baker: *"No, no, no"*

Steven Crowder: *"Okay, let's say, no picture but you can write on it Ben loves Steven forever and have our hands holding."*

Baker: *"No, no."*

Next News Network: *"Steven Crowder, that's his video. It now has over two million views. (Crickets chirping) And what's that the sound of? That's the sound of the gay rights movement responding to that hidden camera video. Where is the outrage against the Muslims? Shouldn't they be on the same receiving end as the Christians?"*

Uh yeah, if you weren't being a hypocrite! But it gets way worse than that. This hypocritical behavior is also within the homosexual community themselves. Let's give it the ultimate acid test. You say I'm guilty of a hate crime, but I don't hate you and I don't advocate violence and you're the one that hates me and advocates violence. You say your definition of love is that I need to accept you and to tolerate you but yet you refuse to tolerate me. Let's say I go to a gay bakery, and I want you to make me a cake that affirms a heterosexual relationship. Surely, they aren't hypocrites, they're going to say of course. No. When they were asked to make a traditional marriage cake, guess what they say? No! Look at this!

"Christian bakers are being punished for refusing to make gay wedding cakes. So, what happens when you ask gay or pro-gay bakeries for a cake that says, 'Gay marriage is wrong?'"

Man on the phone: *"Yes, I'm just searching for a place right now where I could get a cake for our pro-traditional marriage celebration we're going to be having in a few weeks. I was wondering if I could get a cake that says, 'Gay marriage is wrong.'"*

Woman at the Bakery: *"We do pizza sized cookies. No marriage quality type of thing."*

Man on the phone: *"Well, no, it's a celebration for pro-traditional marriage of one man and one woman. We would like to have a cake or even a pie or something that would say, 'Gay marriage is wrong.'"*

Woman at the Bakery: *"Okay, we're a gay cookie shop and I don't think that is going to work."*

Man on the phone: *"I thought you guys were for equality. I mean, what about all the Christian bakeries in California that have been attacked because they refused to make homosexual cakes."*

Woman at the Bakery: *"Okay, we don't even make cakes. We only make cookies, and we are also a gay cookie shop."*

Man on the phone: *"Okay, would you make cookies that say, 'Gay marriage is wrong?'"*

Woman at the Bakery: *"No!"*

Man on the phone: *"Oh, so you guys aren't for equality then."*

Woman at the Bakery: *"We are but why would we support something that is against what we're working towards?"*

Man on the phone: *"So why would Christian bakeries be making cakes for homosexual marriages, yet you guys use the state to force them to do that?"*

He makes another phone call to a different gay bakery.

Man on the phone: *"I am searching around for a cake for a pro-traditional marriage celebration that we're going to be doing soon. I was wondering if I could get a cake that says, 'Gay marriage is wrong.'"*

Woman at the Bakery: *"I apologize, but we don't support that."*

Man on the phone: *"Why not?"*

Woman at the Bakery: *"Because half of our staff is gay. You have a great day!"*

He makes one more phone call.

Man on the phone: *"Yes, this is Columbia City Bakery in Seattle, Washington?"*

Man at the Bakery: *"Yes, correct."*

Man on the phone: *"Right now I am just searching for good deal on a cake for our pro-traditional marriage event that we are going to be doing in a few weeks and I was wondering if I could get a cake that says, 'Gay marriage is wrong.'"*

Man at the Bakery: *"If you can get a cake that says that?"*

Man on the phone: *"Yes."* (The phone goes dead; he's been hung up on) *"Hello."*

Not very tolerant, now, are they? And that was the tip of the iceberg, there was a ton more than that! But, to me, if ever there was a hypocritical behavior, that was it! Not only is that not mentioned in the media either, but again, it shows that this issue has nothing to do with so-called equality. It has to do with the eradication of specifically Christianity and Christian beliefs and Christians themselves from America! And lest you think that's not the case, they even admit it. They want to get us out of the country! Look at what this lady said!

Religious Freedom Fight, Controversy over new state laws. Meet the Press Reports.

Amy Walter, National Editor, the Cook Political Report: *"But here's the tipping point, the tipping point has been reached and that tipping point is done. Which is, this is not an issue in which Republicans can win. They could a few years ago, they can't now. Even when you look at Evangelical younger folks, they have moved on, on with this issue too. So, if we took everybody over the age of 50 and just moved them out of this country, this wouldn't be an issue at all."*

Excuse me? Can I translate that for you? If we just get rid of all you dissenters, all those old-fashioned people with old-fashioned mindsets, like Christians, whatever the age, then this country will be ours! And, no, we haven't moved on this issue, we're being lied to on this issue, we're still 12 to 1. Which means, we're in the majority and it's very concerning to us! So, if we would speak up and get unified on this and get back to Biblical truth, we could turn the thing around.

And if that wasn't bad enough, the Church is also displaying this same level of hypocrisy as well. This duplicit behavior. Stop and think about this. Aren't we doing the same thing when we as Christians say we need to take a stand on traditional marriage and traditional marriage values, but we don't do them ourselves? For instance, we say we need to pray for revival for God to come rescue our nation from this sin. Oh God help us please! But you never pray? You hypocrite! That's not going to help! Knock it off! And yet 20% of professing Christians never pray. And 80% never go to a prayer meeting! Or you sit there and say we need to stand on the Word of God, and that is what we need to get back into our school system, into our government, we need to get back to the Biblical principles, dare I say, that are even the foundation of our Bill of Rights and Constitution that governs our lives and is the source of truth, you need to submit to it, but you don't even pick it up! You hypocrite!

- 25% of professing Christians never read the Bible.
- 50% never go to Sunday School.
- 50% of say there is no absolute truth.
- 55% of professing Christians say the Bible has errors in it.
- Which has now led to 93% of professing Christians no longer having a Biblical worldview.

In other words, you don't even know what the Word of God says, and you sit there and say you're going to stand on it! You hypocrite! Or you sit there and say we need to stick together as Christians and get united on this issue before it's too late, but you never have fellowship with other Christians? You actually forsake the assembly of the brethren. 10% of reported church members cannot even be found.

- 30% never attend Church services.
- 58% don't have being active in a local Church as a top goal in life.
- 75% are never engaged in any Church activity!

Oh yeah, we're united, we're going to win! Are you kidding me? Stop being a hypocrite! This is a part of the problem not the solution! Or finally, you sit there and say we need to share the gospel with these folks so they can get saved and turn around so they can go to heaven. That lady, that doctor, who refuse to learn what a woman is. My heart goes out to them. They need God. That kid that is being brainwashed. That dad that is sitting there, doing that to his kid. They need Jesus Christ. Those people that are clapping in that audience. They need Jesus Christ. Those people who made those cartoons, we need to get the gospel out. Because laws can't change a person's heart, but Jesus Christ can. He's the solution. But you never witness?

- 40% of professing Christians never give to any cause, like sharing the Gospel.
- 47% don't have a commitment to the Christian faith as a top priority in life.
- 70% never give to missions.
- 95% never ever win a soul to Christ.

In other words, we're being a bunch of hypocrites! And if we're ever going to experience revival, we have got to get rid of this hypocrisy. And whatever you do, don't be the worst hypocrite of all and say you support traditional marriage and you're against same sex marriage, but you don't even follow traditional marriage values yourself. You say it's between a man and a woman, and you say it's a solid commitment but violate God's plan for marriage and instead cheat and "test the waters" of marriage before you get married. It's called "living together" or "cohabitation." You're being a hypocrite! The Bible calls it fornication. It's the first one on the list with homosexuality which means it too is a sin!

1 Corinthians 6:9-11 "Or do you not know that the unrighteous will not inherit the kingdom of God? Do not be deceived; neither fornicators, nor idolaters, nor adulterers, nor effeminate, nor homosexuals, nor thieves, nor covetous, nor drunkards, nor revilers, nor swindlers, will inherit the kingdom of God. Such were some of you; but you were washed, but you were sanctified, but you were justified in the Name of the Lord Jesus Christ and in the Spirit of our God."

So, the Bible says homosexuality is not just a sin, but it's mentioned right smack dab in the middle of a list of sins, a whole bunch of sins, that God doesn't approve of, right? Including fornication which is the first one mentioned. You don't get to have your cake and eat it too, Christian. You don't get to drive a car around for free for two years before you make a commitment to buy it. You don't get to live in the house for five years for free without having to pay a mortgage. It doesn't work that way! And neither does it work that way for traditional marriage!

Marriage, and all the things that come with it, including living together in the same house, are only to be enjoyed within the confines with a solid commitment "after" you get married! Not before! This is what God says.

THE BIBLE ON COHABITATION

John 4:16-18: "'Go and get your husband,' Jesus told her. 'I don't have a husband,' the woman replied. Jesus said, 'You're right! You don't have a husband – for you have had five husbands, and you aren't even married to the man you're living with now.'"

Question. Did Jesus condone her lifestyle, or call her on the carpet for it?

Hebrews 13:4: "Marriage should be honored by all, and the marriage bed kept pure, for God will judge the adulterer and all the sexually immoral."

I Corinthians 6:18-19: "Flee from sexual immorality. All other sins a man commits are outside his body, but he who sins sexual sins against his own body. Do you not know that your body is a Temple of the Holy Spirit, who is in you, whom you have received from God? You are not your own."

I Thessalonians 4:3-5: "It is God's will that you should be sanctified: that you should avoid sexual immorality; that each of you should learn to control his own body in a way that is Holy and honorable, not in passionate lust like the heathen, who do not know God; and that in this matter no one should wrong his brother or take advantage of him."

I Thessalonians 5:22: "Abstain from all appearance of evil."

Don't flirt with it, don't even go there! Don't even give the appearance that you're married when you're not! You're lying! You're not only being a hypocrite! It's a sin and it should be avoided, just like homosexuality! In fact, even secular researchers are admitting that cohabitation or living together will destroy a family, not make it stronger.

THE STATISTICS ON COHABITATION

- Cohabitation or living together prior to marriage in the United States has increased by more than 1,500 percent.

- More than 60% of all marriages are preceded by cohabitation.

- Nearly half of 20-somethings agreed with the statement, "You would only marry someone if he or she agreed to live together with you first, so that you could find out whether you really get along."

- And about two-thirds said they believed that "Moving in together before marriage was a good way to avoid divorce."

So, the question is, "Is this true? Did God get it wrong?"

- Couples who live together before marriage (especially before an engagement or an otherwise clear commitment) tend to be less satisfied with their marriage.

- Couples who live together before marriage are more likely to divorce and more open to divorce than couples who do not live together.

- Women are more likely to view living together as a step toward marriage, while men are more likely to see it as a way to test a relationship or postpone commitment.

- The more months couples live together, the less enthusiastic couples are about marriage and childbearing.

- Annual rates of depression among couples that live together are more than three times what they are for married couples and the level of depression rose with the length of remaining unmarried.

- Couples who live together prior to marriage report lower levels of happiness, lower levels of sexual satisfaction, poorer communication, and poorer relationships with their parents.

- The longer couples live together before marrying, the more likely they were to resort to heated arguments, fights, aggression, disagreements, hitting, and violence when conflicts arose.

- Women with live in relationships are more likely to suffer physical and sexual abuse than married women.

- Women with live in relations are nine times more likely to be killed by their partner than were married women.

But what about kids? Is living together good for them?

- Research reveals that, "Commitment and stability are at the core of children's needs; yet, in cohabitation, these two requirements are absent."

- Yet now, 40% of all children now spend time in cohabitation households.

- A 2011 report indicated that children in cohabiting households are more likely to suffer from a range of emotional and social problems, such as drug use, depression, and dropping out of high school, behavior problems and lower academic performance, compared to children of intact, married families.

- Children living in cohabiting households are 8 time more likely to be harmed than children living with married biological parents.

- In fact, the most unsafe family environment for children is now one in which the mother lives with a boyfriend.

- And that's why every empirical study indicates that living together does not produce healthier, happier marriages, or children, but the contrary.

- And research has shown that part of the reason why we see this massive rise for cohabitation, is the Church's failure in teaching the truth about sexuality and marriage.

In other words, the Church is not taking a stand on God's Word, you're being a hypocrite, and you refuse to love people enough to tell them the truth that they're hurting themselves, just like with the sin of homosexuality. Undealt with sin of homosexuality will keep you out of Heaven. And undealt with sin of fornication will keep you out of Heaven.

STOP COMPROMISING
STOP BEING A HYPOCRITE
STOP CELEBRATING PEOPLE'S DESTRUCTION

That is about the most ungodly, unloving, unchristian thing you can do. Here's the good news. The promise made to Israel, secondary application, could it happen to us today? It could. It's happened twice in our nation's history.

2 Chronicles 7:14: "If My people, who are called by My Name, will humble themselves and pray and seek My face and turn from their wicked ways, then will I hear from heaven and will forgive their sin and will heal their land."

What's the word there? Did He say the lost? Did He say the world? Did He say the secular environment? Did He say our country? Did He say these people involved in the things we've been describing? Who's He talking to? Us. My people, God's people who are called by name. Notice how we skip the humble part. Do we need to pray for revival? No, the first thing we need to do is humble ourselves. I'm just quoting scripture. We don't even get that right. And then we need to pray. But what's the context? God, pray, get those people, they need to get their hearts right. No, even if we do pray, we are praying backwards. If we pray and seek His face. Yep, we do it once a year. We need to get around a flagpole and pray. That's it, the rest of you go do whatever. No, you need to seek God's face and then you need to turn from your own wicked ways. Do you get it? It's us that need to get rid of this hypocrisy. If you want to turn things around, it's us.

The church needs to get right with God. Then He will hear us from Heaven and will heal our land. If you think we are too far gone, I'm the proverbial optimist. I don't know God's time frame; I know the planet is headed towards the seven-year tribulation. None of us are going to stop that. But could God possibly, even as bad as it's getting, with the depraved minds everywhere, you think it's too far gone, it couldn't happen to our country. Even if we do have revival, we know it's not going to last forever because the seven-year tribulation is coming. But all I know is that if it is going to happen, we have got to get right with God first. But it can happen, and it can happen with the whole country. And lest you think that that couldn't happen to our nation, then take heart. Listen to what the President of Uganda announced.

President Yoweri Museveni celebrated Uganda's 50th anniversary of independence from Britain at the National Jubilee Prayers event by publicly repenting of his personal sins and the sins of the nation. *"I stand here today to close the evil past, and especially in the last 50 years of our national leadership history and at the threshold of a new dispensation in the life of this nation. I stand here on my own behalf and on behalf of my predecessors to repent. We ask for your forgiveness. We confess these sins, which have greatly hampered our national cohesion and delayed our political, social, and economic transformation. We confess our sins of idolatry and witchcraft, which are rampant in our land. We confess sins of shedding innocent blood, sins of political hypocrisy, dishonesty, intrigue, and betrayal. Forgive us of sins of pride, tribalism and sectarianism, sins of laziness, indifference, and irresponsibility; sins of corruption and bribery that have eroded our national resources, sins of sexual immorality, drunkenness and debauchery; sins of unforgiveness, bitterness, hatred and revenge, sins of injustice, oppression and exploitation; sins of rebellion, insubordination, strife and conflict."*

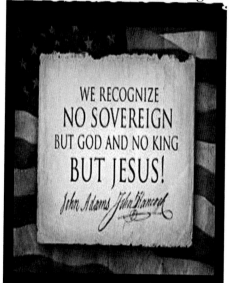

Next, the President dedicated Uganda to God saying, *"We want to dedicate this nation to You so that You will be our God and guide. We want Uganda to be known as a nation that fears God and as a nation whose foundations are firmly rooted in righteousness and justice. To fulfill*

what the Bible says in Psalm 33:12: 'Blessed is the nation whose God is the Lord. A people You have chosen as Your Own.'"

That could be our country, that could be our President, if we turn from our hypocrisy and our wicked ways. God is still on the Throne! He can heal our land. There's always hope. You just saw one President of one nation where it actually happened. That could be us if we get serious! But what about all those skeptical questions, like, "Homosexuality isn't even mentioned in the Bible," or "You're interpreting that wrong," or "Love is love, what's the big deal, etc.?" We'll get to that in the next chapter.

Chapter Eight

A Biblical Response to LGBTQ+

Enemies Within is very current and very applicable to our study of the Book of James, "How to Spot a Phony Christian." This is what's going on and the reason the church is so messed up. We have been looking at the perversion and the twisting of God's truth. The twisting of Biblical love, using eros instead of agapao. Using eros, they say we should allow any and all, sinful behavior. As we have seen in previous chapters, the different ways that God reveals His Biblical love. And personally, I'll take that love over the sick twisted perverted one of today. Which leads us to the next twisting. And is this sick twisted perverted love, correct? No! Absolutely not!

It's now being used to try to justify the 2nd twisting – Biblical relationships. They twisted the rainbow, marriage between a man and a woman and now Pandora's Box has been opened. Now this twisting has led to twisted relationships. Not only homosexuality and lesbianism, but now to polygamy, gender fluidity, pedophilia, and bestiality. Why? Because as God warned when you go down this route, He will hand you over to a depraved mind and you will start doing things that ought not to be done!

In the last chapter we took a deeper look at what this depraved mind looks like. We saw that with …

Depraved Interview
Depraved Ken doll
Depraved Cartoons
Depraved Threat – Hate Crime – Gay Manifesto
Depraved Hypocrisy – Don't go after Muslims – Don't Bake Straight Cakes
Depraved Threat – Want to kick us out of our own Country.
And we the Church need to get rid of our own hypocrisy if revival is ever going to happen!

As was asked before, what about all those skeptical questions like, "Homosexuality isn't even mentioned in the Bible," or "You're interpreting that wrong," or "Love is love, what's the big deal," etc.? Well, before we get into that, let's deal with another aspect. We dealt with the hypocrisy, now let's deal with a bit of irony. For instance, we saw how the Church is not only being silent on this issue, but many professing Christians are even caving in on this issue, they're going right along with it, if you can believe that!

But here's the irony. Non-Christian nations, third world nations, even communist nations are acting more "Christian" than we do. Here's how Russia responded after the Supreme Court ruling.

"Just a week after the U.S. Supreme Court legalized same-sex marriage across America, a historic triumph for the gay rights movement, it seems that Russia won't be joining in the celebrations. President Putin's ruling party has unveiled a straight flag in a bid to combat what it calls gay fever. The group used the country's annual day of family love and fidelity, the Russian equivalent of Valentine's Day to unveil the flag, depicting a father, mother and three children, it contains the hashtag real families. Moscow's United Russia branch says it honors the nuclear family and traditional Russian values. Despite earlier claiming the flag aims to

counter the LGBT rainbow version, the deputy head says it is in no way offensive."

Deputy Andrey Lisovenko, United Russia: *"We aren't saying there is no confrontation here. We are speaking of the traditional family. You can see there are a lot of children here, many elderlies, young people, people on bicycles and rollerblades. We mean the average standard Russian family that is ours as you see illustrated in the logo. Mother, father and three children."*

You know, traditional family. What do you think would happen if we took that traditional family flag that Russia is popping out and we put it up here at Sunrise or somebody's business here in Las Vegas? What do you think would happen? They would go nuts. But this is Russia, a communist nation, that has enough sense to say no. There is no way we are going along with this. In fact, this was recent, this I believe was just two weeks ago.

Russia is now criminalizing LGBT propaganda. Big fines, if you even try to promote this, you're in big trouble with Russia. In fact, I just saw a thing the other day. Japan's doing the same thing. A Buddhist nation. We are supposed to be the Christian nation, and here they are, a communist country acting more Christian than us. In fact, it's getting so ironic that many churches in America are not only caving in on this issue, but they're actually helping it along!

Now, let's move on to the next thing. It's not just hypocrisy, it's not just ironic, this is sick. I'm not making this up, a so-called Christian Seminary called, The Chicago Theological Seminary handed out free condoms at the 2015 Wild Goose Festival. I do have a problem, why are you handing out condoms at a church? But that wasn't the half of it, on

that condom was a gay rainbow flame, mocking the Second Coming of Jesus Christ. Excuse me? Folks, that's blasphemous!

Christian Seminary Handout

Here's Russia saying no, we're going to take a stance; in fact, we will penalize you if you even try to promote this LGBT, and the Church is handing out that. You don't think we have been taken over? Or as one guy said, "Hey, it might be a teensy-weensy bit distasteful to compare the events of the return of Jesus Christ to gay sex." The Church did this! This is not just ironic, it's sick! We better get motivated like Russia, as ironic as it is to say that.

Now let's get to this aspect of the Church not only being hypocritical, but they are also being ironic, and as Christians we're supposed to be truth tellers. The truth is what sets you free. This behavior is a sin and sin hurts, sin harms, and sin destroys. But you hear many Christians say, "Well, my church just never talks about this stuff. And I just don't know how to respond." So, we are just going to respond to the criticism that's out there and we're going to do what the Scripture says. We're going to give it a defense for the hope that lies within us. We are going to answer fifteen accusations from the LGBT community - Biblically. So, we can get equipped, and we can do what the Scripture says. We need to speak the truth in love. If in fact, this behavior is the wide road that leads to destruction, which I believe it Biblically is, then the most loving thing we could do is to love somebody enough to tell them the truth. Now what they do with that is between them and God. But let's get equipped so we can lovingly, effectively as Christians, go around doing that. So, we can say to them, "Have you thought about that Biblically? Have you thought about that logically or philosophically? Because where you are headed is not a good road. It would be the most unloving thing for me to keep my mouth shut.

Many churches and so-called Christians have caved in on this issue. And they've gone so far as to become complacent and refuse to respond or engage in any conversations, towards the accusations made by the LGBT movement, accusing you and I of somehow being non-Christian or unloving like Jesus.

The 1st false accusation we need to respond to is "You're not supposed to judge." Really? What Bible are you reading? That is not what God says! How many of you have heard that one? You should never judge. You just need to tolerate this. This is one of the biggest ongoing lies from the pit of hell. Here's what they're misquoting to suck us into this lie, along with the false teachers and false teaching and cults. They take the Scripture out of context. They actually want to throw the Bible in our face to say basically, "Shut your mouth, you have no right to even speak about my behavior with the LBGT movement."

Matthew 7:1-5: "Do not judge, or you too will be judged. For in the same way, you judge others, you will be judged, and with the measure you use it will be measured to you. Why do you look at the speck of sawdust in your brother's eye and pay no attention to the plank in your own eye? How can you say to your brother, 'Let me take the speck out of your eye,' when all the time there is a plank in your own eye? You hypocrite, first take the plank out of your own eye, and then you will see clearly to remove the speck from your brother's eye."

Well, there you have it. The Bible says we should never judge another person, no matter what they believe, no matter what they say, we just love them and accept them, right? Wrong! That's what people want it to mean, but that's not what it says! In fact, they take it out of context and frankly, that whole passage, that's all they focus on. Here's how most people interpret this passage. That's what you have to do if you're going to come away from that passage and say you're not supposed to judge. That's what you do, scribble, scribble, scribble.

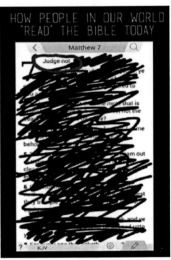

And not only that. That's why we're in the mess we're in. Apparently, this is the version of the Constitution that the Supreme Court read.

"We, the Supreme Court make the laws," uh, uh. I think it's time you throw away your black little highlighter there. And not only that, but this is also how people approach the Scripture. It's not a bag of trail mix. You can't just pick out the pieces you like and ignore the rest. You have to deal with it all. But that's what people do today.

THIS IS NOT A BAG OF TRAIL MIX

YOU CAN'T JUST PICK OUT THE PIECES YOU LIKE AND IGNORE THE REST.

I'm here to tell you this is another one of the biggest lies the enemy has thrust upon the Church in these last days, and certainly with the issue of homosexuality...that we shouldn't judge. That judging is actually a sin or you, calling out their sin, is a sin. It's nuts!

And the reason why I know this is not true, is because if we weren't supposed to judge anyone or anything, no matter what they say, believe, or do, including their behavior of homosexuality, then why did Jesus say this?

John 7:24: "Stop judging by mere appearances and make a right judgment."

Jesus isn't saying we should never judge! He didn't say to never make a judgment. He said when you do judge make sure that it's right! Get your facts straight! He said it right there! And if we're really never supposed to judge, then why did the Apostle Paul say this?

1 Corinthians 6:1-5: "If any of you has a dispute with another, dare he take it before the ungodly for judgment instead of before the saints? Do you not know that the saints will judge the world? And if you are to judge the world, are you not competent to judge trivial cases? Do you not know that we will judge angels? How much more the things of this life! Therefore, if you have disputes about such matters, appoint as judges even men of little account in the church! I say this to shame you. Is it possible that there is nobody among you wise enough to judge a dispute between believers?"

I don't know about you, but it sure sounds like we Christians are not only supposed to be judging, but we're supposed to be judging up a storm, right? That's why sin begins to permeate like yeast. You've got to say something, you've got to deal with it. Five verses, how many times does the word say we're to judge in there? And the context is "us." So, the question is, "Why in the world do people quote Matthew 7 and say we're never supposed to judge? They're quoting it out of context!

Matthew 7 is dealing with a hypocritical judgment where a person's judging somebody of something when they themselves are guilty of doing the very same thing if not worse, like we saw before with fornication. How do we know? Because the rest of the text says that the one person judging has a log in their eye, and the other only has a speck of dust in their eye. But if you read the rest of the passage, it doesn't stop there. It doesn't say don't ever judge. It says first take the log out of your own eye and then you can what? You can rightly judge and remove the speck from the other person's eye! The whole point of the passage, and **John 7**, is to not say that we're never to judge but do just the opposite! It says to get rid of your hypocrisy first, get your facts straight first, so you can make a righteous judgment, right?

It does not say we should never judge between right and wrong.
It does not say we accept everything as right and nothing wrong.
It does not say we just need to tolerate.

And by the way, we've seen this before. Let's get equipped again. This is the other game they play. They don't tell you that they've changed the definition of tolerance. You and I think, well they say you need to tolerate us. We think, well that's kind of like using the Christianese phrase, love the sinner but hate the sin. That's not what it means anymore. In fact, if you say that that's what it used to mean, when it used to be in the dictionary. But that's not what it means anymore. When you say love the sinner but hate the sin, they say that is the most bigoted statement you can make today. Because they changed the definition of tolerance. And here's how they're sucking us into it.

Josh McDowell: *"Some of you say, wait a minute, I thought tolerance was good. That's the problem. Little Johnny comes home from school and* *that very sincere Christian mother from the most fundamental evangelical church meets little Johnny, says, 'Honey, how was school today?' He answers, 'Oh, mommy, we talked about tolerance.' And that Christian mother says, 'Oh, that's wonderful. You know, Jesus taught us to be tolerant.' Absolutely not! That mother is undermining everything she believes, and it won't take years, it only takes months to come back and haunt her.*

Wait a minute, I don't get this. The reason is this. Now there are two distinct separate definitions of tolerance. One I call it historic or traditional tolerance. It's one that almost every one of us here has been conditioned to think by and how you are listening to me through this traditional tolerance. I am speaking from a whole new definition of tolerance. Traditional tolerance would be defined by Webster to bear or put up with someone or something not especially liked. Or in our circles we'd say, 'You know God has called me as a Christian to love the sinner but hate the sin.' That's one of the most bigoted statements you can make today. You make that very statement in an average classroom today and that entire class would turn on you. The bigotry, the intolerance to say love the sinner, hate the sin.

The reason is there's a second definition of tolerance. I would say, Eighty percent of the time, outside the walls of the church, when you hear the word tolerance, whether the media, magazine, school or what, it is not the tolerance you're conditioned to think by. It's a whole new definition of tolerance. Eighty percent of the time it's a new definition. The tolerance you were brought up with is now referred to as negative tolerance. The new tolerance is called positive tolerance. It's defined this way. Every single individual's values, beliefs, lifestyle and claims to truth are equal. Let me repeat that. All values, all beliefs, all truth, all lifestyles are equal. And if you dare to say there's a value of belief, a lifestyle, or a claim to truth greater than another, that is called hierarchy and that's the new definition of bigotry. A bigot today has nothing to do with racism or anything. A bigot today is someone who's committed to moral hierarchy that there's differences in values, beliefs, lifestyle claims to truth.

Positive tolerance adds the word praise. What it means is this. We not only want your permission, we demand your praise. And if you do not praise my value, my lifestyle, my claim to truth as equal to your own, now listen to this, as equal to your own from the heart, you are a bigot, and you are intolerant. From the heart. It's called positive tolerance. Let me show you just how it's hit the church just a little briefly. You tell me historically what's the number one verse that's been quoted from the Scriptures by Christians, non-Christians, Christian young people, non-Christian young people, the media, everything.

What's the number one verse quoted historically by the Scriptures? **John 3:16.** *Do you know what it is now? Have you all been listening to your own young people? Can anyone tell me now how far out front of everything, what's the number one verse quoted even by Christian young people from the Bible? Number one now, what is it? 'Judge not that you'd be not judged.' Listen! Why the moment you make a judgment you're saying there's hierarchy, and that makes you a bigot and intolerant. It makes you stand against the number one virtue in culture tolerance. All is equal.*

Christian love and the number one virtue of culture today cannot coexist. In fact, I'll go as far to say that Christian love is the number one enemy of virtue in culture tolerance. In fact, men and women, I'll say this, I believe now it's a point as a pastor, evangelist, someone like that, it's very difficult to be popular and faithful. Jesus loved that woman at the well and in love and compassion He said to her, 'Go call your husband.' She said, 'Sir, I don't have a husband.' In loving compassion Jesus said, 'That's right. You've had five husbands and the one you're living with now is not your husband.' Jesus exposed her lifestyle. He was witnessing to her. He was exposing her lifestyle. Now speak to me. Did Jesus expose her lifestyle as an alternate, or a sinful lifestyle? You're a bigot. We're right there to say that you're intolerant.

Who do you think you are to have the corner on truth? Like you have the right to make any moral judgment He didn't love. If you don't believe me that's not true. You try anywhere in culture today, you just go one week into the high schools, universities, and Jesus did it in love. Christian love and intolerance cannot coexist. We better wake up."

Why? Because everything we believe in as Christians is at risk! Think about it! Because of this new definition of tolerance they put on us, we're now going to become the new enemy of the state! We have become the worst, biggest, bigots, intolerant people on the planet. All that we believe in, which is what they're using to justify that we are haters, guilty of a hate crime because we don't go along with what they say. And again, we are not the ones making up all the rules. Everything we believe in, all of Christianity, all the Scripture is based on God's hierarchy of right and wrong! He makes up the rules. I'm not making up the rules. I'm just reporting what He said. But their new definition flips it on its head and says everything we believe in is going to become the new enemy of the state. Things we can't budge on as a Christian. Jesus is the only way to Heaven, not one of many. As we saw in our previous study, seventy percent of people claiming to be Christians say there is more than one way to Heaven. Why? Because of this tolerance, the Bible declares that there is only one God; not several or that we can become gods ourselves. And the Bible clearly says that homosexuality is wrong! The very Ten Commandments are all absolute judgments of what's right and wrong from God!

You shall not murder
You shall not commit adultery
You shall not steal, etc.
You cannot tolerate that!

Plus, how can all values be equal? What if someone's "value" was to molest his or her children? Is that right? Am I supposed to accept that? If you bought into the new definition of tolerance, you would have to say yes. Yet, every ounce of your being says NO!

What if it was another person's "value" to teach their children to steal for a living? What if it was a mother's "value" to teach her daughter a fulfilling lifestyle called prostitution? What if a father had a "value" he wanted to teach his son called being an abuser of women? Now can I tell you something? Some religions on the planet today do teach that! They treat women as prostitutes, and they force them into a subservient lifestyle and even kill them if they don't like them. I'm supposed to accept that? In certain religious cultures today, people get their hands chopped off for stealing or their heads chopped off just for disagreeing. Do we agree with that? Should we tolerate that? I don't think so!

It's true Biblical Christianity that's freed people historically from these tyrannous belief systems by setting the standard of right and wrong! We do not tolerate sin in any form! Why? Because sin hurts, sin harms, and sin destroys, and I have to love people enough to tell them the truth about that. Therefore, I have to judge! But in essence it's not me, I'm just upholding God's judgement, I'm just reporting the news of what He says is right or wrong for people's own benefit.

The 2nd false accusation that needs to be responded to is "You're discriminating against me." And my response to that is, "Okay, so what's your point?" The problem with this accusation is they're assuming all discrimination is bad and/or that you don't do it yourself, and that's not true. We all discriminate all the time on all kinds of things.

What kind of foods we eat
What programs we watch on TV
What we will or will not allow our kids to see on TV
What school to go to
What job to get, etc.?

Everyone has a certain criteria by which we discriminate against something. Even bad things, like child molesters. I won't let them hang around my kids, is that bad? I would hope people would discriminate against that! Or people teaching false doctrine from the Bible that's leading others astray. I have to discriminate against that as a Christian. I need to protect them from lies. And disagreeing with homosexuality is not discriminatory in a legal sense as it's being touted, but rather in a spiritual and moral sense. I'm not saying…

You need to get fired from your job
You can't be my neighbor
You can't shop at the same store I do.

Rather, I disagree with you spiritually and morally and currently in our country we have the freedom to do so. This issue isn't discrimination so much as it is you disagree with my spiritual and moral stance on the issue. Which I can do in peace! Plus, if you think about it, the manner in which you disagree with me, by your own definition, you're discriminating against me too! So, what's your point? It makes no sense!

The 3rd false accusation that needs to be responded to is "You're being hateful and homophobic. Now this is one that is constantly thrown in our face to get us into silence, just because we disagree. And as I've already stated, no true Christian is advocating any "hate" let alone "violence" or "bodily harm" to anyone who is involved in this behavior, homosexuality, or lesbianism. And shame on anyone who says they're a born again Christian and they do! Knock it off! This is why we're in this mess! You're giving the rest of us a bad name. But since when is teaching that homosexuality is a sin anymore hateful than teaching lying is a sin, or stealing is a sin, or adultery? How is that spreading hate?

And by the way, true Christians can disapprove and disagree with a behavior and still be civil and loving to the ones with whom we disagree. That's what I advocate, that's what I do as a true Christian. However, liberals and pro-homosexuals do openly express disdain and ridicule against Christians, and it is they along with the media who are guilty of spreading hate towards the Christian community and Christian beliefs. So, is this okay for you to do by your own definition?

Christians are being fired from their jobs.
Teachers are being suspended.
Students are being punished and rejected.
Christian military are being court martialed.
Not to mention Christian facilities being attacked and vandalized.

And by the way, how is disagreeing with this homophobic? There are plenty of people in the world who disapprove of various behaviors like, lying, coveting, hatred, mockery, stealing, pedophilia, etc. Does this mean we now need to label these people "liarphobes," "covetophobes," "hateophobes," "mockophobes," "theftophobes," "pedophilophobes," etc.? And if that's true then shouldn't I call you a "Christianophobe," or a "Bibleophobe?" Think about it.

The 4th false accusation that needs to be responded to is "This behavior is normal." Now, believe it or not, some would say homosexuality shouldn't be considered wrong because it's normal. Well, let's put that belief to the test. The word normal means, "conforming to the standard or common type." Therefore, homosexuality cannot be the normal or standard type of behavior because it only represents less than 3% of the population, and even less in other countries.

1.2% of Australians identify themselves as gay.
1.5% of Britain's identify themselves as gay.
And only 1% of Canadians say they're gay.

That's not the majority which means it is not the normal behavior. It's not the standard! But then some will even go so far as to say, "Well, homosexuality occurs within animals so that means its normal." Really? The premise is what happens in the Animal Kingdom is normal for humans? You really want to believe that? Some animals eat their young, is that good for humans? Is that normal? They also eat other creatures alive, barf up food for their kids, and eat doo doo! Not trying to make fun of anybody, just pointing out the facts. That's not normal human behavior! And by the way, if evolution were true, and it's not, but if it was, then how could homosexuality survive if it doesn't produce offspring? You wouldn't have evolution. Or as one guy puts it…

And again, I don't say that to be mean, it's just because of the facts. If evolution is true, you wouldn't exist. The homosexual community works with the media to bombard us with their pictures trying to get us to think this is normal when it's not.

The facts reveal that homosexuality is not normal behavior, it's a learned behavior. Let's flip those stats around. Here's the normal behavior.

More than 97% of Americans identify themselves as straight.
98.5% of Britain's are straight.
98.8% of Australians are straight.
And 99% of Canadians are straight, which means that (picture) is the norm.

The 5th false accusation that needs to be responded to is "Homosexuals are born that way." How many of you have heard that one? Yeah, it's everywhere, unfortunately even in the Church. The problem is, it's not true! And this can be easily demonstrated in the case of identical twins. If genetics determines sexual orientation, then it should manifest itself in twins who by nature share the exact same genetic information. The problem is that's not the case, and it's a well-established fact! One twin can be gay, and the other is not! How can that be? It means you're not born that way, it's a choice, just like lying, stealing, adultery, fornication, etc. In fact, is that what you're going to do after you rob from a bank and stand before the Judge and say, "You can't prosecute me, I was born this way." Don't think so! And it doesn't work with other sins as well!

And by the way, don't accuse God of going against His character. He's not going to "make people" in a way that contradicts what He teaches. He teaches homosexuality is a sin, like all other kinds of sin, and He's not going to "make them" that way, a "homosexual" or a "thief" or "whatever" and then turn around and condemn them for it. That's not His character. Rather, homosexuality, like all other sin, is a choice and because God's character is good, He lovingly warns them of going down that sinful route.

I've seen people who've made the choice to begin to flirt with going down that route. I've literally watched, within a matter of months, that with that choice, when you start hanging out with thieves, what do you start acting like? A thief. You start hanging out with people who are immoral sexually, what do you do? You start to take that on. If you hang out with a bunch of liars, what do you start doing? It's who you hang out with. And when people start going into that camp, I have literally watched a person begin to change how they talk. Change how they hold their hand. Change their mannerisms. It's a learned behavior. You are not born that way.

The 6th false accusation that needs to be responded to is, "If people love each other so what." How many of you have heard that one? And if that's your basis for acceptable behavior, we've got some problems! For instance, as we have already seen, polygamists say they love each other, right? Does that make it right? Pedophiles say they love that young person and even have the audacity to say that young person loves them. Is that okay? How about bestiality or incest? That's being pushed right now too, under the same premise. They love one another.

If saying you "love each other" is the basis for the acceptance of a behavior, then where does it stop? Rather, God is Love and He Loves people enough to warn them of unloving behavior that hurts people.

The 7th false accusation that needs to be responded to is "Jesus didn't talk about homosexuality." And once again, that's not true either. Granted, He may not have "mentioned" the word homosexuality, but that does not mean He didn't condemn it.

Matthew 10:15: "Truly I say to you, it will be more tolerable for the land of Sodom and Gomorrah in the day of judgment than for that city."

Matthew 19:4-6: "And He answered and said, 'Have you not read that He Who created them from the beginning made them male and female, and said, 'For this reason a man shall leave his father and mother and be joined to his wife, and the two shall become one flesh? So, they are no longer two, but one flesh. What therefore God has joined together, let no man separate.'"

Mark 10:11-12: "And He said to them, 'Whoever divorces his wife and marries another woman commits adultery against her; and if she herself divorces her husband and marries another man, she is committing adultery.'"

John 5:46-47: "For if you believed Moses, you would believe Me; for he wrote of Me. But if you do not believe his writings, how will you believe My words?"

So, here we see Jesus clearly condemned Sodom and Gomorrah, which we know homosexuality was involved in those cities. And we also see Him confirming heterosexual marriage as God's pattern, right? He cites God's creation with Adam and Eve as male and female and even cites divorce within the context of male and female. And He supported the teachings of Moses which contains the **Book of Leviticus** which condemns homosexuality. So yes, Jesus didn't mention the word homosexuality, but He did condemn it, if you're honest with the text.

The 8th false accusation that needs to be responded to is "The word homosexual is not in the Bible." I don't know if you've heard of this accusation before, but it's becoming very, very popular lately. And what people say, is that the word "homosexual" didn't appear in the English Bible until 1946, therefore this disagreement with homosexuality is a "modern biasness" brought on by fundamental Christianity and has only been added to the Bible recently. Well yes, the "word" "homosexual" didn't appear in the Bible until 1946, but that's not because it's not there.

The word as it's used today didn't even enter into our English vocabulary until 1892, long after many English Bibles were printed, including the KJV. And back then it was used to describe a sexual perversion. So naturally it would take this newer word some time to get assimilated into the culture and literature, and the English language, including the Bible, which is why it finally started popping up in the English Versions in 1946. It's just a new word! However, with that said, the Bible clearly mentions homosexuality and condemns it all along because the Greek, which is what the New Testament was written in, not English, clearly talks about it.

It's the Greek word "arsenokoites," which is mentioned in **1 Corinthians 6:9** and **1 Timothy 1:10** and it means, "A man who lies in bed with another male in a sexual manner," i.e., a homosexual as we know today. So, what's your point? It was there all along. And by the way, prior to "arsenokoites" being translated, "homosexual" the newer word, it was translated in English with the word "Sodomites." Referring to the sin of Sodom which again is homosexuality! So again, what's your point? You're just looking for a loophole!

The 9th false accusation that needs to be responded to is "God doesn't disapprove of homosexuality." Now, this one blows me away. If you read the Bible, and I think that's the problem, people aren't reading the Bible. But if you read the Bible, God clearly disapproves of this behavior! How can you even say He doesn't?

Leviticus 18:22: "You shall not lie with a male as one lies with a female; it is an abomination."

Leviticus 20:13: "If there is a man who lies with a male as those who lie with a woman, both of them have committed a detestable act..."

1 Corinthians 6:9: "Or do you not know that the unrighteous shall not inherit the kingdom of God? Do not be deceived; neither fornicators, nor idolaters, nor adulterers, nor effeminate, nor homosexuals..."

Romans 1:26-27: "For this reason God gave them over to degrading passions; for their women exchanged the natural function for that which is unnatural, and in the same way also the men abandoned the natural function of the woman and burned in their desire toward one another, men with men committing indecent acts and receiving in their own persons the due penalty of their error."

So how many would agree, that if God is calling something, "An abomination, detestable, unrighteous, degrading, indecent, a penalty, and an error," He doesn't approve of it, whatever it is. Well, that's what He says about homosexuality and lesbianism. How can you ever say He doesn't disapprove of it is beyond me.

The 10th false accusation that needs to be responded to is "Eunuchs in the Bible support homosexuality." Now, here's where they try to switch gears and actually try to say the Bible supports this behavior that God clearly disapproves of, as wild as that is. And the first one they'll bring up is this passage talking about a Eunuch.

Matthew 19:12: "For there are eunuchs who were born that way from their mother's womb; and there are eunuchs who were made eunuchs by men; and there are also eunuchs who made themselves eunuchs for the sake of the kingdom of heaven. He who is able to accept this, let him accept it."

So here they would say these "Eunuchs" in this passage are talking about "homosexuals" and so we should "accept" it. Wrong answer! A quick look at the context reveals nothing of the sort!

First of all, the context of this passage is speaking about marriage and divorce, which God has already defined as a man and a woman. So, it has nothing to do with homosexuality, number one. Number two, the three Eunuchs Jesus is talking about in this passage is...

One, eunuch from birth, meaning those who were incapable for marriage from some physical deformity that prevented them from having children.

Two, those who were physically castrated, which was a practice in that day for those who took a job of guarding the king's harem, his ladies.

And three, those who chose to be single for the Kingdom of God.

That's it! It has nothing to do with homosexuality, let alone condoning it!

The 11th false accusation that needs to be responded to is **Genesis 2**, "Only talks about a suitable helper."

Genesis 2:18: "It is not good for man to be alone. I will make a helper suitable for him."

And here they would say that God didn't define a marriage partner as strictly male and female but left the door open for a homosexual relationship with the word "suitable helper." You just need a helper. They would say they prefer a "man" a homosexual, or a "woman" in a lesbian relationship and thus this is their "suitable helper." Excuse me? First of all, this is another twisting of the Scripture! God clearly defined who the "suitable helper" for Adam was. Eve, a woman, not a man!

Two, the passage goes on to state the purpose of this "suitable helper." That was to "procreate" i.e., make babies. "Be fruitful and multiply and fill the earth." And you can't do that if you're a homosexual or lesbian. That's not a "suitable helper" for God's purposes. That's not what that passage means.

The 12th false accusation that needs to be responded to is "The sin of Sodom and Gomorrah was gang rape." Say what? Believe it or not, the sin these people want us to believe that God condemned in those cities was not homosexuality but gang rape! And they say that because those that came to Lot's door demanded to have sex with these two men, i.e., the angels. That part was wrong. They were trying to force themselves on them. But if somebody wanted it then it's okay. Say what?? Talk about twisting the Scripture. We already saw what God calls this behavior, "an abomination, detestable, unrighteous, degrading, indecent, a penalty, and an error." So, how can that be acceptable when every occurrence in the Bible indicates homosexuality as a gross sin. Whether it's gang rape or not, individually or corporately? Then they'll go on to say it's really about Sodom and Gomorrah's ill treatment of outsiders and go on to cite an obscure passage in Ezekiel.

Ezekiel 16:49-50: "Now this was the sin of your sister Sodom: She and her daughters were arrogant, overfed and unconcerned; they did not help the poor and needy. They were haughty and did detestable things before me. Therefore, I did away with them as you have seen."

And they say, well you see, God didn't even mention homosexuality here so that wasn't really the sin. Really? Did you notice the word "detestable" there? He's already told us what He considers a "detestable thing," i.e., homosexuality! Yes, they did other sins too, like all sinners do, but that doesn't mean the one detestable sin isn't a sin because it's not specifically mentioned! And by the way, would you really have us believe that your recent and modern reinterpretation of the passage of the Sodom and Gomorrah account is the correct interpretation, when thousands and thousands of Biblical Scholars throughout the centuries and centuries of Church history before you got it wrong? I don't think so! They clearly taught, and have taught for centuries, that the major sin that brought Sodom and Gomorrah down was homosexuality. You just don't want it to be wrong.

The 13th false accusation that needs to be responded to is **Leviticus 18, "Doesn't Apply Today."** And here people would say that the passages in Leviticus, clearly condemning homosexuality, as we have seen, doesn't apply today because that's in the O.T. and we don't live under the Old Testament law anymore. Well, nice try, but let's take a look at that premise. You need to look at what laws apply to today and what don't. Just saying it's in the Old Testament isn't true! Does that mean we get rid of the Ten Commandments? So, something's wrong.

First of all, there were actually three divisions of laws in the Old Testament: Civil, Ceremonial, and Moral. The Civil laws, yes, are no longer in effect, because they expired with the demise of the Jewish theocratic governmental system. This is why we don't put to death the homosexuals, let alone the adulterer, as mentioned in that system when they commit that sin. Nobody's advocating that. And this is why Jesus "freed" the woman caught in adultery, contrary to what the Jewish people did want Him to do. However, He did say, "Go and sin no more."

The Ceremonial laws are no longer in effect as well because Jesus, our High Priest, has fulfilled all the necessary priestly work on our behalf. Which includes the dietary laws, like no eating of shellfish or pork etc. Because they'll say, "Well, the Bible says shellfish is an abomination just like homosexuality and we can still eat shellfish, so homosexuality is okay." No! You're misunderstanding the Ceremonial laws. The prohibition against eating shellfish and pork and all the other foods mentioned in the Dietary laws that are part of the Ceremonial laws are no longer in effect. That's why God gave Peter the vision in the Book of Acts, about now being able to eat all things as being clean, including shellfish and pork.

The Moral laws, like the Ten Commandments, like the moral disapproval of homosexuality and adultery and the other moral sins are still in effect. Why? Because they are based on God's character that doesn't change. And that is why He says in both the Old and New Testaments, "BE YE HOLY AS I AM HOLY," because we're supposed to look like Him and act like Him and behave like Him, and homosexuality doesn't do that! Besides, if you're going to pick out one moral prohibition in the Moral laws and say it's now okay today, then you have to do it for the rest. Which means murder, stealing, lying, adultery, bestiality, incest, and sacrificing children just to name a few would now be okay, if that's your logic. But that would be ludicrous as we both know, let alone dangerous!

The 14th false accusation that needs to be responded to is **Romans 1**, "Speaks of Going Against Your Sexual Orientation." Now this one is amazing. **Romans 1** as we saw before clearly condemns homosexuality and lesbianism. And yet these people would say the phrase there, "natural function" in that passage, is speaking of their "natural orientation" which they say is being gay for them. And thus, they say the "real sin" going on here is not homosexuality or lesbianism but rather going against your "natural desires." Say what? Now you're really stretching things!

First of all, the words are, "natural function" not "natural preference." It speaks of use and not personal desire. And what is man's natural function or use with women according to the Bible? To physically engage in marital sex to fulfill God's command of, 'being fruitful, multiplying, and filling the earth." You can't do that with homosexuality or lesbianism and that's why it's not a natural function, and that's why it's condemned by God.

The 15th false accusation that needs to be responded to is "Homosexuality Doesn't Harm Anyone." And here's where they'll typically say, "Well alright, just leave us alone, maybe you got me on the Bible thing, but what's the big deal, we're not hurting anyone." Really? Actually, that's one of the biggest lies to date. Homosexuality and lesbianism are one of the most destructive behaviors a person could ever do to themselves, let alone the rest of society. Let's take a look at the statistics on this Behavior.

IT HARMS THEMSELVES

- Domestic violence rates are higher among homosexuals, nearly double than the heterosexual population.

- Homosexuals are 50% more likely to suffer from depression and engage in substance abuse than the rest of the population.

- 73% of psychiatrists in the American Psychiatric Association report that homosexual men are less happy than others and they believe their problems are due more to personal conflicts than to social stigmatization.

- The risk of suicide for homosexuals jumped over 200% if an individual had engaged in a homosexual lifestyle and homosexual men are 6 times more likely to have attempted suicide than heterosexual men.

- And this is why the average lifespan of a homosexual is now on average 24 years shorter than that of a heterosexual man.

- Breast cancer rates are higher among lesbians, as well as higher rates of alcohol consumption, smoking, lack of exercise, and obesity.

- Lesbians also have higher rates of psychological counseling and are 3 times more likely to suffer from other compulsive behaviors.

- And historical data has shown that lesbians have a marked increased risk of adverse sexual, reproductive, and general health outcomes compared with heterosexual women.

IT HARMS OTHERS

- Homosexuality can bring huge financial and emotional stress to other people.

- For instance, homosexuals can sue people who are exercising their religious beliefs who can then incur significant financial and emotional stress upon the family, not to mention losing their business.

- For instance, if a Christian orphanage is forced to shut down because of its religious disagreement to turn children over to homosexual couples, is someone hurt in that scenario?

- If a public-school teacher voices their disapproval of homosexuality on Facebook, on their own time, away from work, in their own home, on their own computer, and is fired from their teaching position, are they harmed?

- When morally conservative people who disapprove of homosexuality are labeled as "moral dinosaurs," "bigots," "hate mongers," "right wing fanatics," "preachers of hatred," "intolerant," aren't they being harmed?

IT HARMS SOCIETY

- The push for gay marriage means a redefinition of sexual morality and with that other sexually related practices that are harmful, as we saw, things like pedophilia, polygamy, bestiality, etc.

- A disproportionate percentage, 29%, of adult children of homosexual parents had been specifically subjected to sexual molestation by that homosexual parent, compared to only 0.6% of adult children of heterosexual parents.

- Having a homosexual parent(s) appears to increase the risk of incest with a parent by a factor of about 50.

- And if gay marriage increases and heterosexual marriage decreases, society will be harmed because if we do not produce more children, our society will die. Which means there won't be enough people to support the infrastructure, medical needs, economic development, etc. That is a fact.

- And due to the health risks associated with homosexuality, $12.1 billion dollars are spent annually in health care costs for them, making it a major societal financial drain.

- The homosexual lifestyle is highly promiscuous and brimming with disease and neither is it a "monogamous affair."

- 83% of the homosexual men surveyed estimated they had had sex with 50 or more partners in their lifetime, 43% estimated they had sex with 500 or more partners; 28% with 1,000 or more partners, with only 4.5% reporting faithfulness to the same partner.

- Among married heterosexuals, 85% of married females reported marital faithfulness and 75.5% of married men reported marital faithfulness.

- A recent CDC study found that 1 in 5 homosexuals were infected with HIV and nearly half (44%) were unaware of their infection.

- And worldwide, there are now approximately 1 in every 100 adults aged 15 to 49 that are HIV-infected.

Now, with all due respect, so much for not hurting anyone. You hurt yourself, you hurt others, you hurt Christians, you hurt the economy, you hurt our country, what's next? You really want me to approve of this? I can't! And it has nothing to do with not loving you, it's because I love you! This behavior is not good for you or anybody and that's what the statistics say! I'm not making this up! How can I approve of something like that? That would be one of the most unloving things I could do! And that's why if we're going to respond correctly to this issue of twisted relationships, we have got to do it right this time.

NOT with COMPLACENCY
NOT with SILENCE
NOT with COMPLIANCE
NOT with COMPROMISE

NOT with HYPOCRISY
NOT with CONDONING this DESTRUCTIVE BEHAVIOR
AND NOT with HATE

But love, true love, Biblical love, like Jesus, who loved people enough to tell them the truth. Yes, speak up, yes, get equipped, yes, share the truth, but do it correctly, consistently, and biblically, like this girl did.

Mom is on the phone: *"Well, we're busy as usual. Titus, he's at State. It's his last semester there. And Megan, she's a senior now. Really involved in school and church. Oh, no, it's not school. She does pretty well there. No, it's church that has her running ragged."* Her daughter kisses her mom on the check and walks out the door. *"Bye sweetheart. Be careful."* Back to her conversation. *"Sorry, what, she's been spending a lot of time up there this semester. She goes at least once a week."*

Her daughter is getting into her car to head off to her destination.

"Don't get me wrong, I love that she's passionate, it's just that in the last year she's changed. I'm not sure what it is exactly but she's different. So, last week I asked her why she feels she has to go every week. She is telling me that she is doing what God was telling her to do. I know. You don't think that God would ask her to be so radical though, do you?"

Her daughter has gone to pick up some other kids to take them to the same destination.

"You know we all go to church, right? You know, we are a Christian family. She is really taking this seriously. She's been going to this place for weeks now. You know, it's just not safe."

As the daughter reaches her destination, people are holding up signs saying, "God hates fags" **"Jude 1:7"** "AIDS cures fags" **"Romans 1:27,** read it." She walks up to the people holding the signs.

"My daughter has the ability to do whatever she wants. She's got to understand that people, they're going to start forming their own opinions. I just think she's not thought through the implications. You know, it's probably just a phase. You know like when she did cheerleading or piano lessons. How long can she go on like this? I don't know where she gets it. Certainly not from me. She just has to be different."

Her daughter, along with the friends she picked up, walk into the hospital room to see a patient in bed. They hold up the signs that they have drawn to show him. One sign says, "We love you" and the other sign says, "We're praying for you." The patient has a big smile on his face, and they gather around him laughing and loving him.

I have witnessed to a lot of people, I've witnessed to a lot of people in the occult, like I used to be. I've witnessed to a lot of people who were drug addicts, I've witnessed to people who were adulterers, lying thieves. In Sacramento we used to go witness to men who were dying at the AIDS Hospice. These men weighing 70, 80 pounds, I don't know how much time they had left, but you know what? I didn't hold up a sign that said, "God hates you." I didn't say, what you're doing is perfectly fine. We went there in love and said "God loves you, it's not too late. You still have breath. Turn to Jesus. He can forgive you of adultery, lying, stealing, drug abuse, homosexuality." That's how we witness.

"If My people, who are called by My Name, will humble themselves and pray and seek My face and turn from their wicked ways, and love like that, not condoning, not hatred, not saying God hates you. But in love, telling them the truth, praying with them, leading them to Jesus. Then I will hear from heaven and will forgive their sin and will heal their land." Let's Get It Right this time. We may not get another chance. If there's any hope for our nation. Amen?

That's how we respond to these twisted relationships.

How to Receive Jesus Christ:

1. Admit your need (I am a sinner).

2. Be willing to turn from your sins (repent).

3. Believe that Jesus Christ died for you on the Cross and rose from the grave.

4. Through prayer, invite Jesus Christ to come in and control your life through the Holy Spirit. (Receive Him as Lord and Savior.)

What to pray:

Dear Lord Jesus,

I know that I am a sinner and need Your forgiveness. I believe that You died for my sins. I want to turn from my sins. I now invite You to come into my heart and life. I want to trust and follow You as Lord and Savior.

In Jesus' name. Amen.

Notes

https://enemieswithinthechurch.com/
https://get.dailywire.com/wiaw/subscribe?utm_campaign=wiaw&utm_me
dium=paid&utm_source=bing&utm_content=na_subscriptions&cid=wiaw
&mid=b&xid=0&utm_term=matt%20walsh%20what%20is%20a%20wo
man&utm_campaign=&utm_source=bing&utm_medium=ppc&hsa_acc=6
411461344&hsa_cam=429594023&hsa_grp=1326012504412860&hsa_ad
=&hsa_src=s&hsa_tgt=kwd-82876595724471:loc-
190&hsa_kw=matt%20walsh%20what%20is%20a%20woman&hsa_mt=e
&hsa_net=adwords&hsa_ver=3&msclkid=56252383adbb12cecfaa403665
7a0a84
http://bible.crosswalk.com
http://www.bible.org/illus/h/h-25.htm)
http://www.sermons.org/hell1.html)
http://www.worldofquotes.com/topic/Hell/1/)
http://www.anzwers.org/free/lastwords/)
http://www.anzwers.org/free/lastwords/)
John MacArthur, Jr., *The Love of God*
(Dallas: Word Publishing, 1996, Pg. 146)
http://www.strato.net/~w5mav/wisdom/crucifixion.htm)
http://www.bible.org/illus/c/c-156.htm)
http://www.pastorshelper.com/wwjd/wwjd1.html)
http://www.holmescountyherald.com/1editorialbody.lasso?-
token.folder=2004-04-07&-token.story=79053.112112&-nothing)
http://www.bible.org/illus/g/g-70.htm#TopOfPage)
http://www.bible.org/illus/g/g-70.htm#TopOfPage)
http://www.bible.org/illus/o/o-01.htm#TopOfPage)
Roy B. Zuck, *The Speaker's Quote Book*,
(Grand Rapids: Kregel Publications, 1997, Pg. 236)
John MacArthur, *Commentary on the Book of Romans 1-8*,
(Chicago: Moody Press, 1991, Pg. 392)
http://www.bible.org/illus/m/m-15.htm#TopOfPage)

http://www.bible.org/illus/m/m-15.htm#TopOfPage)
http://www.bible.org/illus/m/m-15.htm#TopOfPage)
http://www.bible.org/illus/g/g-49.htm#TopOfPage)
Roy B. Zuck, *The Speaker's Quote Book*,
(Grand Rapids: Kregel Publications, 1997, Pg. 383)
https://www1.cbn.com/cbnnews/us/2016/june/southern-baptist-convention-supports-mosque-draws-criticism 2/4 worship
http://http://www.economist.com/blogs/erasmus/2016/06/buildingmosques-america
https://www.healthline.com/health/different-types-of-sexuality
https://www.gotquestions.org/pedophilia.html
https://www.google.com/search?q=definition+catamite&rlz=1C1RXQR_enUS939US939&oq=definition+catamite&aqs=chrome..69i57j0i22i30l9.3530j1j7&sourceid=chrome&ie=UTF-8
https://www.reddit.com/r/changemyview/comments/hvz0sj/cmv_zoosexuality_is_a_valid_sexuality/
https://www.youtube.com/watch?v=-WpPYJljV7o
https://www.dshnyc.org/staff-and-storytellers
https://www.youtube.com/watch?v=H_wewFd29Qo
https://www.youtube.com/watch?v=Tb1B3Xbe3LI
https://www.huffpost.com/entry/gary-hall-national-cathedral-homobia-is-a-sin_n_4057614
https://www.youtube.com/watch?v=tcrfeukScK8
https://www.youtube.com/watch?v=gTYL0LtaghE&t=4s
https://www.facebook.com/prophecywatchers/videos/amazing-sulfur-destruction-of-sodom-and-gomorrah-discovered/546085916926061/